ART DECO
ARCHITECTURE
IN NEW YORK

"ART DECO ARCHITECTURE IN NEW YORK"

1920··1940

DON "VLACK"

Photographs by
Ralph Appelbaum

ICON EDITIONS

HARPER & ROW, PUBLISHERS

NEW YORK, EVANSTON, SAN FRANCISCO, LONDON

FIRST EDITION

Designed by Janice Stern, Bruce Stern

ISBN: 0-06-438850-6
LIBRARY OF CONGRESS CATALOG CARD NUMBER: 74-6577

FOR NANCY, NICKY, NINA, ALEXIS, AND NEW YORK CITY

CONTENTS

ACKNOWLEDGMENTS

The idea for this book came to me in Europe, 1972, while looking at the architecture of De Klerk, Van Der Meij, and Kramer in Amsterdam and Pavel Janák and Josef Gočar in Prague. I would like to thank them then, *in absentia,* for their inspiration. I am indebted to my close friend Charles A. Platt II for his encouragement and perception. Cass Canfield, Jr., provided invaluable criticism and advice from his deep store of experience. I would like to thank the following building managers and directors who granted permission and gave assistance in photographing interiors: Thomas F. List, Barbizon-Plaza Hotel; Joseph Gerns, Chrysler Building; Eugene Schmidt, General Electric Building; Robert Reed, Rockefeller Center; Patricia Roberts, Radio City Music Hall; David Elovitz, the Swiss Center. Special thanks are extended to D. Emerson Phelps of Irving Trust, who was sympathetic and enthusiastic from the outset. I am indebted to Elbert Severance of the Chanin Building, a man of encyclopedic knowledge of the Deco era, who opened his memory to me with patience and kindness. To Cornelius Dennis of the Municipal Building Division Archives, my appreciation for his assistance and explanation of building indexing. I wish to thank Dian McDonough for many long hours spent in researching the building archives and Janelle Naylor for her expert and thorough typing of my manuscript. I would also thank Chris Kraemer for his masterful ability to dodge and burn a negative into an extraordinary print.

Finally, I thank my wife for her excellent criticism, forbearance, and devotion which kept me fresh and persevering throughout the writing of this book.

PREFACE

The purpose of this book is twofold.

First: It is intended to be a critical and analytic examination of the relationship between art, as expressed through architecture, and style. New York architecture of the 1920s and 1930s is eminently suited to this type of examination, not only in the traditional sense, but mainly because the nature of the style is basically a parody of the art, and this relationship is rare, if not unique, in architectural history.

Second: From a purely historical point of view, this period needs to be recorded and documented. The conformation of the skyscraper, individually and in concert with other buildings, forming the skyline of the cityscape, is one of the few indigenously American phenomena. New York City is, of course, the primary example. The grid pattern of the city plan is, in the high-rise building, finally made three-dimensional. The logical, open-ended, expansive American sense of growth and optimism is extended from the horizontal to the vertical.

New York City is a dynamic city, and as such is continually destroying and rebuilding itself. The American urban architectural ethic here is mainly concerned with economic growth and progress; consequently the idea of historical preservation is innately illogical, and this is particularly true in New York City. Only relatively recently, in the last ten or fifteen years, has there been a concerted concern with city-planning which could be implemented in a realistic sense. The salvaging or incorporation of historically viable buildings is being considered in relationship to a larger overall pattern. Nevertheless, the Art Deco building is particularly discriminated against. With 1930s architecture, one possible reason (albeit an arbitrary and mass psychological one) for this unconcern is that to a large extent the memory of the depression is so negative that any massive reminder of the time is best eliminated. Aside from the obvious sociological onus of penal corruption, the Women's House of Detention (fig. 1) was a superb example of Deco architecture. The bas-relief of the cast-iron, bronze-patinated spandrels was not only archetypical of the style but also had a special grace and integration. The placement on a difficult site and the proportioning of the mass were exemplary. Moreover, the short row of half-circular ersatz balconies emerged in a reverse cascade from the entrance with distinction. Compare the same device used on the façade of 310 East 55th Street (fig. 2) in order to see how ineffectual it can be. The Women's House of Detention was demolished in 1973. There was a small and eventually futile outcry against its demolition. The Jefferson Street Courthouse, which occupies the same block complex, had been converted into a library in 1967 and has taken on a new interior life—still, however, wrapped in its Mad King Ludwig trappings. This point is brought up only to emphasize the priorities in reclamation.

Most of lower Manhattan has been rebuilt in the past twenty years. Of the three fine examples of Deco office-skyscrapers on John Street, only one retains its original lobby. While the Chanin Building on Lexington Avenue and 42d Street is basically intact, the elevator cabs have been stripped and refinished in Formica. (The enormous irony is that remodeling is done in the name of modernization.) Almost all of the great imposing movie theaters are gone, as are the small shops, being the most susceptible to change. The interior of the Mercedes-Benz showroom on Park Avenue was remodeled in 1972, and Frank Lloyd Wright's original appointments and Deco furniture (he was perhaps the greatest designer of furniture in this idiom) was replaced by, ignominiously, pseudo-Miesian décor. The situation is the same throughout the city.

An interesting and telling indication about the status of Deco architecture is that, at the time of this writing, not a single Deco building is a landmark. There are a number of landmark buildings done during the 1920s and 1930s: Federal, 1920; Italian Renaissance, 1924; Neo-Georgian, 1930; English Georgian, 1930; and English Regency, 1932. One can only assume that these buildings received landmark distinction for some arcane historic reason; certainly there can be no aesthetic justification.

The overriding concern of this book is with preserving these Deco buildings ("preserving" used in the sense of documentation and awareness) not so much for their actual artistic value, which is eventually anachronistic, but as the incredible stylistic expression of an artistic sensibility which is at once clear, original, and particularly American.

New York City contains many hundreds of Art Deco buildings of virtually all types and for virtually all functions. This book is not a comprehensive catalog; many examples are not included. Rather, it attempts a selective description, in text and illustrations, of significant examples of Art Deco architecture in terms of style, function, decoration, and aesthetic interest and importance.

Don Vlack

August, 1974

2

Fig. 1   Women's House of Detention

Fig. 2   310 East 55th Street

1

INTRODUCTORY DEFINITION

The term Art Deco was, as is well known, coined as an abbreviation of "Exposition des Arts Decoratifs et Industriels," a Parisian Design Fair of 1925. In general usage Art Deco almost entirely refers to the traditional sense of *objets d'art* or artistic artifacts ranging from clothes, fabrics, jewelry, and furniture to advertising, books, and appliances. Indeed, every artifact of daily use came under its design auspices.

In the recent literature about Art Deco, architecture plays a very minor and often misplaced role. In many cases, buildings are included within the definition which do not belong by the standards which I will further explain and define. Critics have tended to treat the subject of complex structures with the same deference given a coffee urn by Puiforcat. There is a certain rationale for this viewpoint, since the overt manifestations of the style are similar in both cases, and one might successfully argue that generally Puiforcat was the more complete artist when compared with any minor Deco architect. However, in those instances when the architectural style flowered in its full and complex exuberance, such as in the Chrysler Building, comparisons with the minor arts touch on only one small fraction of the total concept. Architecture is, after all, both an exterior and an interior experience, one which has a great many complicated extensions. It has a demanding quality requiring not only physical participation but various depths of perception as well, and in the best of its examples it generates excitement and awe. In any case, other terms, such as Style

Moderne or Modernistic architecture, perhaps do have a more dignified connotation and might seem a more apt label for the architectural style. But the term Art Deco has become such a definite stylistic category by this time that it would only confuse issues to change the designation.

Chronologically, Art Deco architecture in New York City refers to a certain and specific type of building style prevalent during the period 1920 to 1940. There is some discrepancy in the exact dating, but the years between the First and Second world wars are the usually accepted boundaries. This gives a little temporal leeway in either direction, and while there is no building described prior to 1922 and the most concentrated construction of the twenties decade began in 1925–1926, there are two Deco buildings with dates as late as 1941. In a later section, the special contribution of Frank Lloyd Wright is discussed separately. He did not fit into a stylistic chronology. Also certain distinct aspects of Deco style continued throughout the Second World War, especially in the design of war matériel (the Lockheed P-38 airplane and the Panzer tank, for instance). Domestic building, however, virtually came to a standstill. By 1947–1948 a different architectural framework prevailed.

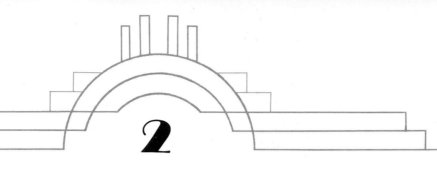

2

EXTRA-ARCHITECTURAL
IMPETUS

HISTORICAL ANTECEDENT: The Art Nouveau

From between about 1890 and 1914 the predominant advanced artistic style was the Art Nouveau or Jugendstil, as it was known in Germany. This style, because of its concern for a special organic (usually plant-oriented) foundation, rarely was able to investigate large-scale construction. Of course there were some exceptions: those designers whose innate sense of engineering was able to transfer a basically energetic yet two-dimensional development into a gravity-viable and supportive structure. Some of the later work of Antoni Gaudí incorporated such sophisticated and innovative engineering concepts that Le Corbusier was moved to consider Gaudí a man of extraordinary force, faith, and technical capacity: a great artist. Also, some of the underpinnings of Victor Horta's buildings were based on difficult and complex principles. In furniture, although chronologically earlier, Michael Thonet discovered that the strength of wood could be increased (through technology). This revelation came to fruition when the new-found strength of bent wood could be transferred into the sinuous Art Nouveau configurations and could also support weight.

These structural developments were actually outside or, rather, beside the mainstream of the movement. The Art Nouveau was primarily a decorative or ornamental style, and whatever structural requirements were necessary were supplied by the most traditional means and materials. It was a sculptural style and as such had little or no need for complex technology to achieve its aims. (Paradoxically it was not until the widespread un-

7

derstanding and use of reinforced concrete that the soul or spirit of organic large-scale sculptural form could be exploited in its fullest sense. Pier Luigi Nervi, Felix Candella, Eduardo Torroja, and, in a roundabout way, Frank Lloyd Wright, and the late work of Le Corbusier and Marcel Breuer have definite roots in the Art Nouveau.) The buildings of Hector Guimard, Henry Van de Velde, Victor Horta, or early Wright for that matter were traditional structures and used traditional materials (with the exception of a modified cantilever—there is still the internal chain construction supporting the overhanging roof line of the Robie House in Chicago—or the frequent use of cast iron).

The artistic concepts of the Art Nouveau were organic and opulent, widely accepted as an outgrowth or partner of eclectic Victorianism (Gothic, Moorish, and so on), and finally antimachine, and thus strongly ego-centered. The Art Nouveau slipped into its historic place so well because it was a time-oriented stylistic mode, and not because it was intrinsically sound structurally. That is, the style had to do with sociological phenomena directly, which are pervasive and eventually acceptable on a popular level. Its most prevalent architectural showcase was the interior (the combinations of *objets d'art*) or the façade, where the fluid decoration could be applied. At times, when it was structurally feasible, certain buildings had the conformation of the objects or the decoration, generally disguising the basic construction.

As a transitional style, and particularly with the use of its motifs and ideas in American building, the Art Nouveau had a limited influence in New York City. One of the first architects to incorporate the Art Nouveau ornamental sensibility (probably independently from concurrent European sources) in an indigenous structural framework was Louis Sullivan. He was at once strongly rooted in the precepts of Chicago School structure (indeed, he was its greatest exponent) and also obsessed with the proliferation of the most delicate organic decoration. Sullivan's one New York City building illustrates the almost contradictory premise—at least in the sense outlined above and which was generally true in Europe—of having a structurally viable, yet Art Nouveau decorated and integrated, tower (Bayard Building, fig. 3). This building and the Baptist Church on 64th Street (which is more Art Nouveau in overall outline rather than decoration and actually is transitional between Nouveau and Deco) are the only two Art Nouveau type of buildings in New York City, and they are distinctly American versions.

It was not Art Nouveau architecture, such as it is, which influenced the Art Deco, but manifestations of the style *in toto*. Historically, then, the Art Nouveau style literally set the stage for the development of the next performance. For the most part the motifs for Deco ornamentation and form were in contrast to or in rebellion against the organic and natural configurations of the Art Nouveau, especially the French and Belgian types. The Scotch, German, and Dutch versions

Fig. 3 Bayard Building

have a somewhat more geometric basis.

There is still a more evolutionary relationship between the two styles. From the morose, drooping posture of the mermaid springs the shoulders-back stance of the nymphet; the sinuous and twisting tendrils and calla lilies give way to the fresh, sprouting stalks of gladiolus and birds of paradise. The lithe and streamlined follow the indolent and languid. Borzois, greyhounds, horses, and eagles are the new pets and replace the snakes and dragonflies. The interest of the Art Nou-

veau was in its mysterious, often sinister iconography, and the vitality of the movement was in its unreleased potential. The whiplash, considered one of the primary symbols of the Art Nouveau, was always in suspension. It was the Deco assimilation which finally snapped the whip by passionately embracing the machine and technological power, and thereby released the latent, crackling energy therein.

There were other similarities between the styles. Esoteric cultures influenced both: the pre-Raphaelites and Moors, Aztecs and Mayans from the Americas, and Assyrians and Egyptians. Rare and expensive materials play an important role in the development of both styles. However, in the Art Nouveau the materials remain traditionally natural (or simulated natural): Tiffany glass, bronze or doré, semiprecious stones or onyx, mother-of-pearl or rare woods. Deco materials range from natural in conjunction with machine-made to newly invented; again rare woods, but plastics, primarily Bakelite, frosted or blue glass, chrome or polished bronze, and finally tiles or mosaics. These comparisons and similarities between the two movements have to do with an emotional frame of reference or point of view as well as with a distinct visual linkage. As was noted above, New York City has no real Art Nouveau architectural background. Consequently the relationship between the two movements is based on their stylistic and emotional continuity rather than any definite or actual example.

9

CONTEMPORANEOUS DEVELOPMENTS: Music, Literature,

Film, Painting, Sculpture

The radical developments in modern serious music provided additional stimuli for Deco concepts. In Europe the invention of twelve-tone structure by Arnold Schönberg and its extension by Alan Berg and Anton von Webern, plus the extreme dissonance and contrapuntal rhythms of Igor Stravinsky, supplied in visual terms serial repetition of motifs on the one hand and aggressive broken rhythms on the other. In America Charles Ives was breaking new ground with the same innovative fervor, if not the critical interest. As difficult and sophisticated as his work is musically, certain aspects of it, particularly his collage effects with existing folk and sometimes national patriotic themes, had a definite public appeal. Likewise, this special confluence of American symbolism (the eagle, for instance) in the general scheme of Deco design is a continuous and recurring aspect of Deco architecture.

Jazz, one of the few authentically indigenous American art forms, perhaps contributed more directly, musically, to the Deco style than its serious counterparts. In its best forms (that is, its primarily black origins) it was an underground music. By 1927 the so-called swing style was in gestation in New York, and its link with popular taste, while never quite proper, was nevertheless ubiquitous. By 1935–1936–1937 the swing style was the popular dance music and, while certainly diluted or transformed by the big bands, disseminated the effects of the original sources on a mass level.

The syncopation and thrust of jazz were also mirrored in the refractive and irregular yet symmetrical (the metrical beat) use of—as one example—the architectural stepback and the peculiar grace notes of the friezes which accompany them. Music donated some of the primitive aspects of the style: that part, in the best work, under the streamlining, which gave it vitality and power.

During the middle 1920s and into the 1930s there was an interest in serious science-fiction writing. This can be seen by the tremendous popularity of H. G. Wells's 1923 book *Men Like Gods* and E. R. Burroughs's innumerable fantastic *Chronicles*. On a more direct graphic, yet more common, level there was the advent of Buck Rogers and Flash Gordon.

The concept of future worlds as various utopias was beginning to flourish and influence visual thinking (for example, Wells's *The Open Conspiracy,* 1928, and Yevgeni Zamgatin's *We,* 1922). The influence was largely thematic and indirect but impactful. Frank Lloyd Wright's 1934 proposals for Broadacre City were utopian in concept, emphasizing a rural, horizontal, gardenlike plan. Le Corbusier's projects for the Radiant City, 1930–1936, and the Plan Voisin for Paris, 1925, had an idealistic and socialistic preoccupation, but his solutions centered on vertical, high-rise, urban structures, which in a realistic sense were at least more attainable than the Wrightian back-to-the-earth romanticism, which ignored the premium value of real estate. It was I. Chanin, one of the greatest Deco architects, who actually conceived a utopian scheme for mass living in the 1930s which was workable. Green Acres in Long Island was the result. Although not built until after the Second World War because of economic reasons, it remains a satisfactory solution to concentrated large-scale housing.

None of these projects or proposals approximated the visions of the science-fiction or utopian writers. They were not the crystal and glass, prismatic, multileveled dreams of the Emerald City of Oz. It was only in the movies that the concepts were realized, because it was only this medium which could take a model or set of an unreal city and make it seem real. While the *Wonderful Wizard of Oz* was written by L. Frank Baum in 1900, the movie was not released until 1939. *Metropolis,* by Fritz Lang, 1926, showed the utopian city to be mechanistic and populated by human robots as envisioned by the Expressionist designers Otto Hunte, Erich Kettelhut, and Karl Vollbrecht. The sets for Lang's *Dr. Mabuse* were by Otto Hunte and Stahl Urach. The sets for Paul Wegener's film *Der Golem* of 1915 were designed by Hans Poelzig, an Expressionist architect. From the New Bauhaus in Chicago (the Institute of Design) László Moholy-Nagy did the models, lighting effects, and designed backgrounds for *The Shape of Things to Come* in 1936.

Since there was no need for a functional or operational structure, the designers could play with and extend the forms with impunity. They could stretch as far as their imaginations would take them. If the science-fiction writers provoked the most fantastic, unreal, and unbuildable images, it was the architect-designer who could at least render these images visually through the medium of film.

The advent of Cubist spacial and formal invention began to have a marked affect on architectural thinking as early as the 1920s. Fernand Léger met Le Corbusier, for instance, in 1921. The ferment caused by this development in painting involved many allied fields of the art world. While Paris was the hub of the movement, its principles spread across Europe, as far east as Czechoslovakia, where Franz Kupka was the leading proponent. In the West, Cubism had its American practitioners as well. The 1913 Armory Show in New York introduced the advanced European Cubist style to America. The show was something of an artistic scandal, so much so that the communications and news media devoted widespread coverage to criticism and analysis.

Max Weber, Arthur Carles, Alfred Maurer, and Patrick Henry Bruce are some of the early American Cubist painters. Niles Spencer, an American expatriate, did very individualistic Cubist painting in England. Morgan Russell was involved with the

Fig. 4 Bronze Screen. Chanin Building

1. Simultaneous vision/comprehension: overlapping planes to define space; fragmentation of solid form to indicate structure.

2. Simplification of natural forms to the geometric triad: cone/cube/sphere.

3. Collage devices: real objects juxtaposed with designed ones.

4. The subservience of color to form.

5. The suppression and diffusion of iconography; all parts of the surface are equally charged and related.

Futurism was a style discovered and promulgated in Italy. The leading painters and sculptors of the movement were Umberto Boccioni, Giacomo Balla, Gino Severini, and F. T. Marinetti. Chronologically, it was roughly concurrent with Cubism. Although there are many similarities between the two movements, there are three or four differences which are crucial.

First, Futurism was a narrow, political, revolutionary style, and its message needed to be proselytized. From a design perspective this political urgency expressed itself in aggressive composition, strident color, extreme asymmetry approaching vertigo, and theatrical exhibitionism of both materials and technique (such as the use of sequins or mirrors as a collage device). Cubism was restrained, introverted, involved with its own forms, quietly turning and reflecting themselves, fitting into compositional place.

Second, the subject matter of Futurism dealt with dynamic, violent nature or nature in flux. Storms, lightning bolts, erupting volcanoes, tidal waves, rearing horses, or straining dogs were some of the content of the Futurist manifesto. The

Cubist movement indirectly through Orphism. Charles Demuth and Charles Sheeler concentrated on the industrial landscape in a manner not unlike the later Purist version of Cubism.

Without delving too far into the deeper painterly or conceptual theories of Cubism, it would be beneficial to review those precepts pertaining to architectural interests. The following is a list of those Cubist innovations which are representative of the method and style:

12

other major subject interests were industrial and technological, including roaring trains, streaming airplanes, racing cars, dynamos, electric generators, and power plants.

Cubist subject matter was completely traditional and bourgeois. The two popular themes were the age-old portrait and the homely still life.

Third, the extraordinary concept of representing objects in motion was achieved by the repetition of overlapping translucent areas of the same figure in the direction of the movement and sometimes back again. The speed of the object is increased in relationship to the blur or numerical increase of the overlapping planes. This method of indicating movement was perhaps known from the photographic studies of Eadweard Muybridge or Thomas Eakins. At least it was technical proof that an object in motion is a different image from one stopped for a split second in time. The dynamic quality of Futurist technique was inescapable, and it had an integrated interrelationship with the violent and straining subject matter. Ironically, this Futurist dynamic concept was popularized in America by a Frenchman, Marcel Duchamp. His *Nude* (traditional subject matter) *Descending a Staircase* was the cause célèbre at the Armory Show. Strictly speaking, this painting is basically Cubist in temperament. Of others outside the Italian milieu, the Russian Kasimir Malevich best understood the dynamic concepts and painted extraordinary Futurist paintings in the 1920s.

Cubism was never interested in violence, speed, or visible thrusts of energy.

Fig. 5 Bronze Screen. Chanin Building

The Cubist concern with multiple images related to exploring all the possible design aspects of the subject matter's innate personality. The fact that the traditional background is spacially integrated with the subject and given as much importance increases the limits of the entire picture plane.

The Futurist artist modulated his entire picture plane also, but it was the supercharge halation of the definite subject matter thrusting, pushing, lunging, or racing in eight or ten directions at once that

Fig. 6   60 Wall Street Tower

Fig. 7   Bankers Trust Ceiling. Nassau and Pine Streets

Fig. 8   200 Park Avenue

was the hallmark of the style. Clashing color and the agitated, hashing brushwork (adapted from Impressionism) further removed the Futurist visual impact from Cubism. Finally Cubist weight was evenly distributed, shifting yet gravity-prone, which held the composition tightly in place. Futurist composition was spinning and twisting in space with élan and verve.

The polished bronze sculpted convector screens of the Chanin Building (figs. 4, 5) employ every Futurist device with such gusto that they are visually explosive. The architectural relationship to Cubism and Futurism depends on how well the designer could extract decorative elements from the theoretical basis of both movements. Light in sequence (60 Wall Street Tower, fig. 6; bank ceiling, fig. 7) is one way to use a repetitive motif in extreme perspective to simulate movement. The brash complementary color combinations used in the polychrome decoration of 200 Park Avenue (fig. 8) give a sense of jumpy rhythm.

15

Fig. 9   Starrett-Lehigh Building

Fig. 10 Empire State Building

Fig. 11   Port of New York

Probably the one Futurist idea most prevalent in Deco architecture is movement, and the way it is best expressed is through glass. Generally, windows are treated as a linear element, either horizontally, using the ribbon window (Starrett-Lehigh Building, fig. 9), or vertically as a column (Empire State Building, fig. 10). This window treatment forces the eye to move along lines of continuous direction with considerable speed. It was the artistic discretion of the architect to adjust and direct that speed in relation to the total design.

The Cubist element of simultaneous planes is found in practically every massive warehouse block (Starrett-Lehigh Building, fig. 9). The changing scale and setbacks of numerous angles and facets (Port of New York, fig. 11) shift in what seem like arbitrary relationships, but the symmetry of the building is such that it is understood that one aspect of a building section is a mirror image of another around a corner (Bell Telephone Building, fig. 12). This assumed expectation reinforces experiencing the building as a totality. It is a particularly needed modulation of form considering the massiveness of the area involved.

18

Fig. 12   Bell Telephone Building

Fig. 13   Apartments on 20th Street

Fig. 14   Apartment on 9th Street

Fig. 15   Apartment on Bennett Avenue

On a smaller scale, low-rise (that is, generally no more than twelve stories) apartment blocks deal with Cubist massing on a simpler level. The repetition of square and rectangular elements, punctuating and interrelating as negative spaces, gives a unified yet varied rhythm (apartments on 20th Street, fig. 13).

The concept of collage usually manifests itself either in surface texture or through the addition of an integrated device such as a fire escape (apartments on 9th Street and Bennett Avenue, figs. 14,

15). Another ironwork addition which acts as a protective screen is the grillwork over ground-floor windows.

Texturally, there were a number of factors involved with breaking up surfaces: brick with stonework (Abraham and Straus, fig. 16) or laid in different color courses (low store with ziggurat pattern, fig. 17); brickwork and metal (Daily News Building, fig. 18); elaborate brickwork (Western Union Building, fig. 19); brick with carved stonework (1939 Grand Concourse, fig. 20).

20

Fig. 16   Abraham and Straus

Fig. 18   Daily News Building

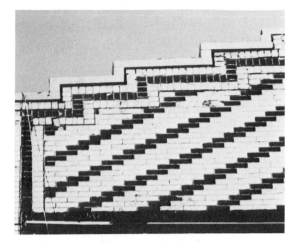

Fig. 17   Lexington Avenue and 58th Street

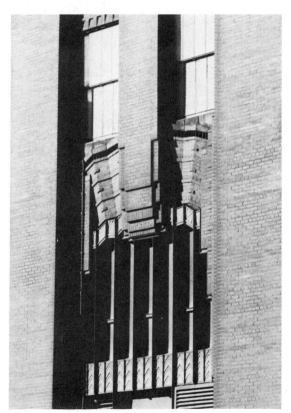

Fig. 19   Western Union Building

Fig. 20   1939 Grand Concourse

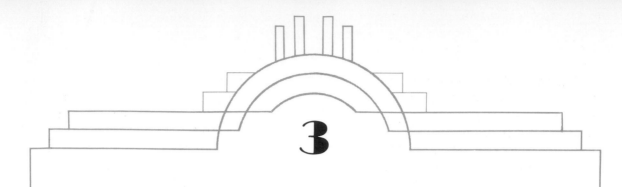

3

THE ARCHITECTURAL IMPETUS

THE INTERNATIONAL MOVEMENT

The twenty-year period from the early 1920s through the 1930s produced some of the most revolutionary architecture ever known. It was not only radical structurally, but also, because of technological developments, radical historically. Structurally there was a break from the confines of masonry construction with the advent of reinforced concrete (ferro-concrete), large expanses of glass, high-rise elevators, steel cage construction, the cantilever, and myriad other technological advances. These innovations, in large part, affected or determined the form of architecture, and the technological possibilities developed a philosophy of building which was unprecedented. Of course sociological factors also contributed extensively to the development of the new architecture: in Europe, a greater feeling of academic/scientific freedom and a sense of the necessity to rebuild after the First World War. In America, the democratic ideal of order and equality of the grid town plan, for example, can be seen as the two-dimensional precursor of the high-rise steel skeleton.

In any case, the modern movement or International Style (its more familiar designation) became as definite in its precepts and rules as any manifesto. One of the tenets of the movement had to do with ornamentation and/or decoration. There was to be none, in the older sense of embellishment or elaboration. The structure was to reveal itself as much as possible through the way it was constructed, and that alone was enough. Anything which detracted from the essential structure was unnecessary and therefore superfluous.

Those earlier structures which were then most admired (in America for example) were exactly those not considered architecture at all. They fell more or less in the category of industrial engineering: silos, large train depots, bridges, cast-iron warehouses, and so on.

The break in Europe from earlier and eclectic modes was relatively swift and defined. There was a more gradual and evolutionary transition from the then avant-garde but diminishing movement of the Art Nouveau. Peter Behrens was more or less the catalytic agent for the dispersal of the newer attitudes, and Le Corbusier, Walter Gropius, and Mies van der Rohe all studied or worked with him. The Bauhaus became one of the great gathering places for the development of a particular design philosophy. The integration of the arts with machine and industrial culture was the format of the school. The Bauhaus had a mission, and to the extent that it affected, in the long run, all aspects of design to this day, the mission was successful. Gropius was a powerful and influential teacher. It was basically his momentum and thinking which gave impetus to the dissemination of the International Style program. Meanwhile, Le Corbusier was working on actual residences and on large urban projects which would have revolutionary repercussions. He was also writing and publishing profusely. Other French architects, Robert Mallet-Stevens and Andre Lurcat, were prominent in the movement; and Lurcat carried the style to Corsica with his Nord-Sud Hotel of 1931. The International Style was far-reaching and spread as far as Russia (I.

Nocolaiev and A. Fissenko) and Japan (Mamoru Yamada). Of course Germany seemed to be the most prominent in the movement, and such men as Mies van der Rohe, Marcel Breuer, Otto Haesler, and Mart Stam are well known.

From the Scandinavian countries came Alvar Aalto, J. J. P. Oud, E. G. Asplund, and Sven Markelius. Czechoslovakia was represented by Otto Eisler and Ludvik Kysela. Spain, Italy, and the United States were involved only peripherally. Richard Neutra, William Lescaze, and the early work of Edward Stone (the original Museum of Modern Art) are examples. In 1931 the Museum of Modern Art gave an exhibition to these forerunners and proponents of the International Style which solidified their position as a definite and potent influential force. Knowledge of the development of the style had been filtering into the United States gradually but consistently prior to this time. In a sense it is rather the concept or theory of the architectural style which was so effective (that and America's natural economic competitiveness), not any actual visual stimulus. Herein lies a paradox. The International Style propounds as part of its design philosophy the express denial of applied decoration—and yet it probably affected the decorative/ornamental thinking of the Art Deco style.

The qualities of the International Style in its decorative transition, however, fall prey to that one conceit all styles do—the transition from art to style being, in this case, extremism. In an architectural sense, then, there are as factors in the International Style: (1) simplicity, (2) asymmetrical balance (from Cubism and De Stijl), (3) function, (4) surface. These factors interrelated and integrated define the architecture. But of course and obviously, ornamentation has no need of this integration. It has no raison d'être especially in terms of its own architectural definition; consequently it must assert itself, it must be more than itself. To illustrate this point compare any of Mies's stainless steel and leather chairs with their chrome and plush counterparts in Radio City Music Hall. The Art Deco style, then, is parasitic, feeding on its various sources, with the major one being the International Style, and flowering into its themes—assuming that its products represent its inspiration when in actuality they mimic it. The Deco style finally (as most artless styles) can be dated by its manner rather than by its content, and as such depends upon history for its artistic justification.

EXPRESSIONISM AND THREE ARCHITECTS:

Sant' Elia, Mendelsohn, Wright

Apart from the more spiritual or theoretical influence of the International movement as a whole was the more powerful voice of the concurrent wave of architectural Expressionism in northern Europe and the single voice of Sant' Elia in Italy. From the United States the gradual magnitude of Frank Lloyd Wright flashed back indirectly or circuitously from Europe, as his earliest work was highly appreciated there.

The German Expressionist architects were concerned with freeing the internal life forces and structuring those energies in their most dynamic manifestation, architecture. Hans Poelzig was perhaps the most powerful architect of the movement, and his chemical factory at Luban and the Grosses Schauspielhaus, a theater, utilized architectural elements which became standard Deco devices. The columns at the theater are perfect examples of the reverse ziggurat, and while slender and elegant, they are not unlike the exterior columns of the Downtown Athletic Club arcade. The Taut brothers, Hans Scharoun, and Hugo Haring were others involved with a more than usual heavy-handed dynamism. Bruno Taut used glass extensively, including glass blocks in various combinations. His prismatic designs precluded many of the faceted wall and spacial treatments of windows (the small numerous panes of most Deco windows, each set fractionally out of sync, create a shimmering refraction when hit by sunlight). The upper tower of the skyscraper project (Friedrichstrasse, Berlin, 1921) of Hans Scharoun bears a distinct resemblance to the tower of Metropolitan Life at Madison Square Park in New York. Hugo Haring's works also contributed extensively to the flow of Expressionist ideas filtering into the United States. Both Hans Scharoun and Bruno Taut entered the Tribune Tower Competition of 1922 with designs which espoused Expressionist canons. The empathic relationships and confluence of ideas were such that Scharoun's entry (except for a certain nervousness of drawing) could easily be mistaken for an early sketch by Erich Mendelsohn.

The other major faction working with Expressionist ideas was the so-called Amsterdam Phantasts. Piet Kramer and Michel de Klerk were the two foremost exponents of this eccentric style. Using traditional building methods (mainly brick), the architecture tended to have a heavy, ponderous quality. Even, and consistently, the window framing was thick wood and invariably painted white so that rather than a spacial element, windows became more a two-dimensional ornament (this is found in Mendelsohn's Einstein Tower as well). The Dutch architects were familiar with Wright's work as early as 1911, when he had an exhibition in Amsterdam, and felt a certain sympathy with his ideas. How well the Dutch architects were known in America is speculative, but considering the international sophistication and interaction in the field plus the close-knit interest in Europe itself, the roots and yearnings were planted everywhere.

There is a critical misconception regarding Deco architecture in France, Germany, and Czechoslovakia. Robert Mallet-Stevens, Gabriel Guevrekian, Andre Lurcat, Boris Kupka, and, obviously, Le Corbusier, Gropius, and early Breuer are not Deco architects. The International Style, which was discussed earlier, separated elements of pure architectural interest, namely spacial modulation, structure as form, and asymmetrical balance based on a real understanding of the precepts of Cubism (Le Corbusier was also an early Cubist painter) from the concept of architecture as a stage set, a backdrop for a specific mood, a sensation rather than an actual aesthetic perception. At their best, International Style architects were artists and as such created timeless works of great aesthetic value in its fullest sense. At times there was a slipover into the self-indulgence of Deco manipulation. Both Guevrekian and Mallet-Stevens, particularly in the relationship with interior and exterior spaces, were sometimes guilty.

Usually, at its best, Deco architecture can only be a definitive example of its own style.

There are rare, singular occasions when the style is perfectly and magically knit with spacial, structural, and formal values. As with all aesthetic analysis, and especially with the most complex form of architecture, there remain certain unanswered questions. In this particular instance pertaining to Deco style, all that can finally be said is that the exception proves the rule. In those cases the result is an awesome architectural statement. Three buildings fall into that category: Rockefeller Center (1931), the Schocken Department Store (1927), and the Johnson Administration Buildings and Research Tower (1936–1939).

Antonio Sant' Elia was an Italian Futurist architect who built only two buildings in his lifetime. He was primarily a theorist who made literally hundreds of drawings and plans of grandiose projects. No aspect of modern, industrial, urban life escaped him. His visionary concepts flowed and became the basis for an environment, vast and mechanically complex. Train depots, hydroelectric plants, dams, and factories were his subjects. The dynamic quality of his studies was not that dissimilar from the German visionary architects. His ideas tended to be less scratchy than Bruno Taut's but also less direct than Mendelsohn's. Sant' Elia's buildings seemed to be the actual power sources of energy—the repositories of action and movement. The Studio per una Centrale Elettrica, 1913–1914 (fig. 21), and the Studio per un Ponte, 1914 (fig. 22), have a resemblance to the George Washington Bridge. The dry-cell battery fins atop the Century Apartments' twin towers also have a reference to Stazione d'aeroplani e treni Ferroviari, con funicolari e ascensori su tre Stradali, 1916 (fig. 23). The demolished Women's House of Detention also owed much to Sant's Elia's vision.

Erich Mendelsohn, too, was an experimental designer. During the First World War he made innumerable Expressionist design-studies for buildings not unlike Sant' Elia's in inspiration. That is, he designed housing for the new industrial, communications, and power stations which he took as source material. These drawings became famous, although only one, in a slightly modified form, was ever

Fig. 21   Studio per una Centrale Elettrica

built: the Einstein Tower at Potsdam. As powerful as this building is, it has more of the character of the culmination of an earlier sensibility. The contoured, organic fluidity of the overall design relates more to the sculptural quality of Jugendstil rather than to Deco. The brashness of spirit and the building's scientific function, so well expressed in the astronomical dome, however, would probably indicate that the building was transitional. It was partly this visionary phase of Mendelsohn's work which influenced Deco architects. The large and important commissions following the Einstein Tower were

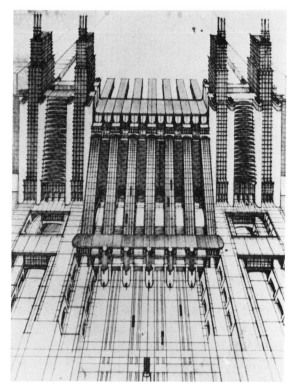

Fig. 22 Studio per un Ponte   Fig. 23 Stazione d'aeroplani e treni

probably the major breakthroughs, setting the mold or rather the superstructure of his life's work. The Schocken Department Stores of 1926–1929, the Metal Workers' Union of 1929, and the Universum Theater of 1928 were five important buildings of this period. An interesting similarity exists between the Petersdorf store of 1927 (fig. 24) and Louis Sullivan's Carson, Pirie and Scott Department Store in Chicago of 1904 (fig. 25). They both have a three-unit drop from the roof line after the sweeping curve of the corner. Also the deep-set window treatment of the 1927 Schocken store in Stuttgart echoes Sulli-

van's classic Chicago window even to the point of having a fixed central pane. There are, however, certain differences which contrast Deco formulations with International Style into a successful amalgam which has great originality. Sullivan's building is firmly rooted to its site, primarily as a result of the even and systematic weight of all the window bays. It also originally had quite a heavy cornice which further compressed its weight. Both the Stuttgart Schocken store and the Petersdorf store have extreme emphasis on ribbon windows with almost invisible reveals. Consequently, there is an enormous velocity shot into the horizontal banding. The buildings seem to be on the verge of takeoff and so embody perfectly the concept of dynamism. The Look Building, the Starrett-Lehigh Building, and the corner of 22d Street and Broadway attempt to emulate this principle. At best they approximate it. In any case, Mendelsohn's influence was far-reaching. He was at once elegant and strong, refined yet inventive; finally he was able to merge successfully a static form with energy and movement.

Frank Lloyd Wright was a supreme romantic and explosively egomaniacal. The anonymous character of the International Style infuriated him, and he was an avid opponent. One of the many aspects of his work was to often elevate the Art Deco style into the realm of Architecture as Art. As a matter of fact his art carried certain ornamentation to heights often sought by the best stylists but never reached. It was because his idea of structure as an organic whole was so all-encompassing that it included not only the complex inner skeleton of a chambered nautilus but the unseen iridescence of the shell and finally the mottled patterns of its surface as well. He insisted, for example, on designing specific furniture and appointments for specific spaces. Each place had its own nature, and as such each part was to be designed in relationship with every other part, and all within the confines of the total concept. Wright and Sant' Elia had a certain ebullience in common. Compare Midway Gardens in Chicago, 1914 (fig. 26), with Stazione e treni (fig. 23). In many cases Sant' Elia, Wright, and

Fig. 24　Petersdorf Store

Mendelsohn converged in point of view. It was, at least, the spirit of dynamism which imbued their work.

As a champion of geometric decoration and effusive textural concern, Wright had formidable power. Here, after all, was a giant whose ornamental ideas could be used in the name of modernity. While the New York architects felt at home with his vocabulary, they could not really cope with his grammar. Basically his architecture was concerned with horizontal structures. The major exceptions to this rule

30

Fig. 25 Carson, Pirie and Scott

turned when it came to construction. His ornamentation was another matter.

Since Wright's individualistic style had more or less coalesced and become codified by the 1930s and 1940s, there was little or no change until his death. Consequently, New York City had to wait until 1959 to receive one of its finest Deco buildings, the S. R. Guggenheim Museum. It is more than an example of a style (which had dissipated by the end of the Second World War). For one thing, it is probably the only building done since 1940 with applied decoration, perfectly integrated with the cornice of the auxiliary office building. The geometric glazing of the translucent glass of the dome is gracefully proportioned, and the ironwork of the exterior gates (fig. 27) continues variations of the basic circular theme, which is used as a module throughout the building. Finally there is the floor grating and bas-relief eagle in the foyer (fig. 28). In the museum structure itself we have the principle of organic dynamism, which is evident from the exterior, transferred to an actual participatory experience on the interior. One experiences the grandiose space and the art while being involved as an actor, governed partly by the spacial relationship (the building as a separate organism), partly by the individual arbitrary relationship with the Art (man as free will), and, ultimately, partly by the invisible, unconscious pull of gravity gently—the slope is only three degrees—leading down and around (Wright's hand as artist-creator). In this great building, movement becomes part of the structure.

are the Johnson Wax Tower, the H. C. Price Co. Tower, Bartlesville, Oklahoma, and the Mile High Center project. But the solutions to these are applicable to very specific vertical problems. There was no way to transfer or exploit the individuality of his particular vertical concept. The New York architect was forced by economics to build structurally simple and tried buildings; to provide the largest amount of space in the smallest area. The only way to go was up. There was no room to experiment with the spacial concepts of Wright. It was to the International Style that the New York architect re-

31

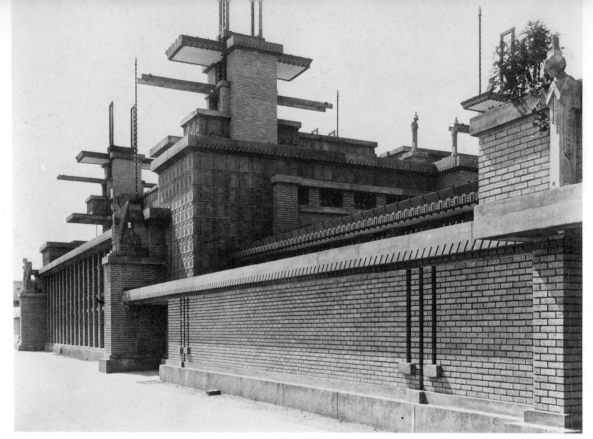

Fig. 26   Midway Gardens

Fig. 27   Exterior Gates. Guggenheim Museum

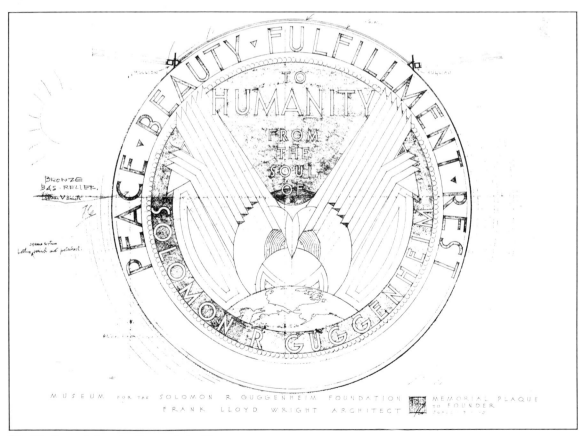

Fig. 28   Bas-relief eagle. Guggenheim Museum

4

DECORATIVE MOTIFS AND SYMBOLS IN ART DECO ARCHITECTURE

FLORA/FAUNA AND MAN/MACHINE

While the overwhelming percentage of Deco motifs are geometric and nonobjective, derived from either the engineering concepts of the architectural style itself or symbolically from scientific ideas, there was another source for the decoration: a direct reference to plants—including ferns, succulents, and flowers—and to animals, fountains, man, and machines.

In almost every case the floral or animal forms were abstracted and, wherever repeated, as in the frieze format, schematized as allover pattern (Chanin Building, fig. 29); Furniture Exchange, fig. 30). There were a few flowers which were used repeatedly: lilies of the valley, hollyhocks, sunflowers, anemones, and finally the two favorites, calla lilies and gladiolus, because they were the most slender and elegant. Leaves were the broad-

based variety rising to a Gothic point, or fernlike and growing from each other. Often the profusion of flowers was anchored in an abstracted fountain theme; the spray of water evenly and precisely curled on either side of a central axis. This vertical division ranged from the capital of a column (bank on Upper Broadway, fig. 31; to the capping of a window rise (Beekman Tower Hotel, fig. 32; 181 Madison Avenue, fig. 33).

There is a certain fashionable or modish quality associated with such highkeyed floral emphasis. Sometimes a great delicacy is achieved in the attenuation of curved and flowing patterns. The perfumed aestheticism is such that a reference to this phase of ornamentation is known as "the French Manner." It can be assumed that what is meant is a continen-

Fig. 29 Chanin Building

Fig. 30 Furniture Exchange, 200 Lexington Avenue

Fig. 31 Manufacturers Hanover Trust

Fig. 32 Beekman Tower Hotel

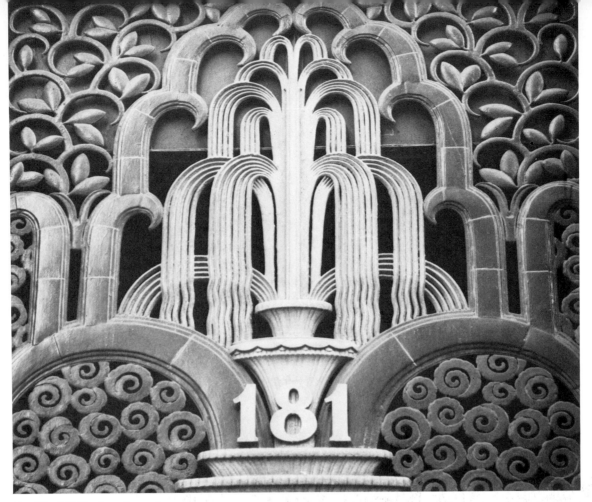

Fig. 33   181 Madison Avenue

tal savoir-faire analogous to kissing hands
upon introduction.

The Art Nouveau era possessed a rich
background of floral decoration and the
opulently tiled and polychromed office
building on 14th Street and Seventh
Avenue (fig. 34 is a rare example of
the transitional change from Art Nouveau to Deco). The floral and ribbon ornamentation at the lower and cornice levels
still retains a slight flavor of the whiplash
and sinuous linear quality of the Art Nouveau. Interspersed throughout, however,
are the strong diamond shape and other
abstract geometric motifs casually assuming equal or more importance.

On a still different and grander level
(241 Central Park West, fig. 35), the large
high relief sprouting ears of corn or perhaps wheat chaff is used architecturally
to pull the columns upward and finally
cluster them at the stepped-back roof
line so that the entire building acts as a
gathered cereal bouquet. This method is
used even more successfully (336 Central
Park West, fig. 36) where the soft, undu-

lating papyrus-fringe has both a kinetic and a unifying effect.

Other uses of floral motifs include actual baskets of flowers (Porters' on Madison Avenue, fig. 37; old New Yorker Hotel, fig. 38). Still another way to incorporate a floral design is over a doorway (740 Park Avenue, fig. 39). A linear lunette of interlaced yet symmetrical gladiolus, their oversized stamens curling toward each other, fills the area gracefully. This spiraling device, either turning inward, as in this instance, or, as is more usual, outward away from the center, is prevalent whenever (7 Gracie Square, fig. 40) an architectural element needs termination (columns), extension, or fill (spandrels, friezes, railings, or ironwork borders).

Animals (Prospect Park Zoo, fig. 41), the recurrent eagle (East River Savings Bank, fig. 42; Airlines Terminal, fig. 43), seagull and dove (Port Authority, fig. 44), seagull (El Dorado, fig. 45), occasionally lions (Temple Emanu-el, fig. 46), and even rats (Graybar Building, fig. 47) play less of a role as decoration for two reasons. Even in low relief this type of more natural association detracts from an integrated decorative point of view. Man (usually nude) as a symbol of strength—the bulging musculature is part of an idealization (60 Wall Street, elevator doors, fig. 48; 90th Street and Fifth Avenue, Church of the Heavenly Rest, fig. 49; Fuller Building, fig. 50)—is neglected for the same reasons. The use of natural figures, however, stylized in the round (Health Building, lamp, fig. 51), tends to make separate entities of the forms which bear little or no relationship to the decorative tone of the building. There

are some exceptions that are not very successful but at least do not interfere with the continuity of the façade. Animals and man were difficult to abstract in the Cubist or at least in the most radical analytical Cubist sense. The reason for this was that strict Cubist form was of course not decorative, having neither a symmetrical nor a two-dimensional basis. The so-called Deco Cubist abstraction leaned more to an amalgam of classical idealism and monumental muscular delineation (Atlas, Rockefeller Center, fig. 52). The whole package was angular and postured.

This idealization satisfied the need for an innate generative strength and was also a neat concentration of mythic power into bourgeois sensibility. The gods-in-workclothes syndrome promulgated by almost every piece of decorative art at Rockefeller Center is probably the best example of this rationalization and gradually became the official sculptural style of governmental commissions. It was also the style of Nazi Germany and persists today in its social realist context in China and the U.S.S.R.

Along with the symbol of man as power are the tools and machines he uses: transportation, such as cars and ships (Greek Shipping Line, fig. 53), communications such as radio-telephone, and energy (the topmost section of the Century Apartments resembles an electromagnetic dynamo, fig. 54). The spires of the Empire State Building (fig. 55), the Riverside Museum (fig. 56), and the Waldorf Astoria (fig. 57) are the as yet undeveloped but known nose cones or tail sections of science-fiction rockets, complete with fins. Construction engineering, scaffolding, and derricks (the triangular bracing of the stair rails of 60 Wall Street Tower, fig. 58) resemble guy wiring or the catenary suspension system of the George Washington Bridge (fig. 59).

These, then, are two major symbols infusing the Deco inspiration: Nature and the Machine. It is man's regulation, control, and finally spiritual domination over both which determine the patterns and forms of the architecture.

Fig. 35   241 Central Park West

Fig. 34   14th Street and Seventh Avenue

Fig. 36   336 Central Park West

Fig. 37   Porter's, 691 Madison Avenue

Fig. 38   New Yorker Hotel

Fig. 39   740 Park Avenue

Fig. 40   7 Gracie Square

Fig. 41   Prospect Park Zoo

Fig. 42 East River Savings Bank

Fig. 43 Airlines Terminal

Fig. 44 Port Authority

Fig. 45 El Dorado

Fig. 46   Temple Emanu-El

Fig. 47   Graybar Building

Fig. 48   60 Wall Street

Fig. 46 Temple Emanu-El

Fig. 47 Graybar Building

Fig. 48   60 Wall Street

Fig. 49   Church of the Heavenly Rest

Fig. 50 Fuller Building

Fig. 51   Health Building

Fig. 52   Atlas, Rockefeller Center

Fig. 53   Greek Shipping Line

Fig. 54 Century Apartments

Fig. 55   Empire State Building

Fig. 56   Riverside Museum

Fig. 58   60 Wall Street Tower

Fig. 57   Waldorf Astoria Hotel

Fig. 59   George Washington Bridge

GEOMETRICS

The most important and ubiquitous motif of Deco design is the ziggurat. This shape is the major theme of Deco ornamentation and manifests itself in hundreds of permutations. The ziggurat shape is elemental, basic, and emotionally satisfying. It is simply the piling of successively smaller and recessive blocks, one upon the other: a very primitive yet solid solution to expansive structure (99 Wall Street, fig. 60; 80 Broad Street, fig. 61). The shape, however, has an aspect which is dynamic; a steady rhythmic or jagged ascension. Some of the historical sources of this shape have previously been mentioned. Owing in large part to the 1916 zoning law, the capping off of a high-rise tower in stepped-back fashion seemed eminently gratifying and practical. The two-dimensional ziggurat shape which became so representative then was to a great extent derived from the exigencies of the three-dimensional architectural form. The ziggurat's enthusiastic acceptance as decoration was probably fixed in extra-architectural ways as well.

One of the major animal symbols of the period was the eagle. There was an enormous amount of governmental building during the depression, and the eagle is, of course, the main national symbol. Again, the Deco eagle, this time grasping a swastika, was the national symbol of Nazi Germany and, with two heads, imperial Russia and ancient Byzantium. From a design point of view there is another and more important factor involved with the eagle. With outstretched wings or wings in a three-quarter outstretched position (which is the usual case) the feathers naturally form the pattern of an inverted ziggurat. This becomes more emphatic when the anatomy is geometrically stylized (East River Savings Bank, fig. 42; Airlines Terminal, fig. 43) in a manner of elegant, monumental, yet ersatz Cubism. This inverted motif in turn forms architectural members which are structural (the columns of the arcade of the Downtown Athletic Club) or, as a negative space, an entranceway (Salvation Army Building, fig. 62), the form now naturally assuming an arch. These forms had other precedents: Aztec temples, Mesopotamian arches, Assyrian colonnades and doorways, Moorish domes and plasterwork decoration, and finally Egyptian mastabas. The earliest culture to develop the form was the Sumerian. The interest in the ziggurat, its sources and influences, conscious and unconscious, fed and reinforced itself in a round robin of design (Sofia Warehouse, fig. 63; 261 Fifth Avenue, fig. 64; Film Center, fig. 65; Brooklyn Bank, fig. 66; clock, fig. 67).

Another aspect of the ziggurat shape was its transformation into arcs. If the recessive stacking of cubes had a solid structural base for a transference into two-dimensional ornament, there was no such basis for the clustering of progressively smaller arcs or spheres about a central axis. The reference here seems to relate rather to a stylized cloud formation

Fig. 60   99 Wall Street

or simply a softer variation on the right-angle step pattern.

There is the possibility that the dome structure of early Byzantine or Islamic religious building may have had some esoteric and unconscious influence. It would, though, be in a reverse structural order system: smaller supporting hemispheres or squinches gradually increasing in size and complexity of vaulting to eventually support the largest hemispheric expanse or central dome. The spiritual aspect of this arrangement is circular and continuous, directly relating to religious experience. The Deco arc ziggurat likens itself to a mass of foamy bubbles flowing from some magical bubble pipe and in decreasing volume. Any underlying spiritual reference would be pagan or Bacchanalian. A bunch of grapes, again inverted, the shape of a curvilinear ziggurat, is a familiar symbol in Deco ornamentation (church gate, fig. 68; staircase, Barbizon-Plaza Hotel, fig. 69). In any case this circular permutation is found frequently. To indicate the pervasive interrelationship between this ziggurat form as structure and the shape as ornament, the outstanding example is the dazzling apex of the Chrysler Building (fig. 70). The three-dimensional angular strength of the stepback is modified and rounded into the

58

ascending and diminishing arcs of the tower, which are stabilized by triangles of glass—a revelation of bracing, culminating in a flashing silver spire.

There is another purely linear aspect to the ziggurat. One of the major Deco symbols is the thunderbolt or the lightning flash. In scientific description, this phenomenon has no definite or repeatable configuration, being an electrical charge of stupendous energy between a constantly variable source and a fixed ground. It can be seen as an instantaneous flash of light which shoots through the sky in angles where there is the least atmospheric resistance. A lightning flash looks most like a denuded tree branch or an X ray of a simplified nervous system. It is the afterimage or the idea of energy which is remembered rather than the actual event. Perhaps because of the primitive power of natural lightning and the fact that man was able to harness electrical energy, the bolt itself was destined to become a visual symbol. It had only to take on a definite form. Inasmuch as the angular and jagged linear progression of the ziggurat had no real beginning or end, but did have the correct energetic rhythm, it was inevitable that the indefinite electrical image should assume *that* conformation (staircase, Chrysler Building, fig. 71). The structural right angles had only to be modified into connected acute angles in order to increase the velocity and force of the symbol (RKO Coloseum, 181st Street and Broadway, fig. 72). If a multitude of lightning bolts are connected, they form a vibrating grid (Western Union Building, fig. 73).

Radio as well as the movies were the two principal forms of entertainment during the depression. Both depended on and grew out of scientific invention. Radio was powered by electricity which generated waves of invisible, mysterious energy, filling the air with crosscurrents of radiant pulsations. It was not too great a leap to turn the vertical lightning bolt on its side and visually duplicate the rhythm of radio energy. (There is also a resemblance to brainwave patterns found on an encephalogram, which was invented in 1929.) This repetition of rising and falling, yet continuous, linear triangles was used especially as frieze decoration in a pseudocornice and as a band between ground level and the second story. This visual energy could wrap itself about a building and define its parts as well (210 East 68th Street, fig. 74). Actual wave patterns are found in Deco ornamentation, being a faster, less ragged rhythm (Gracie Square, fig. 75). In many instances the two motifs are interlaced (22d Street and Second Avenue, fig. 76; hotel, fig. 77).

Still another motif related to the ziggurat variations is the radiating scalloped half-circle. Structurally this motif has the same root as the ziggurat. The symbolic source lies elsewhere. Another aspect of the design makes it dissimilar from our familiar counterpart. Until now every variation of the ziggurat has been strictly symmetrical. The motif can be stretched, condensed, reversed, made circular, or abstracted, but its parts remain even on either side of its axis. Since one of the inspirations of the radiating half-circle is

Fig. 61 80 Broad Street

the sunrise and the other is a central energy source such as a microphone, the beams of light or sound waves can dissipate at uneven or arbitrary lengths. When these arbitrary lengths are connected, usually by arcs, sometimes by triangles, the resulting pattern need not be symmetrical (spandrel of the Health Building, fig. 78), even though they are confined within a proscribed architectural framework (Chanin Building, fig. 79; Irving Trust Building, mosaics, fig. 80). These variations on the sunburst theme are the exception in Deco ornamentation.

The fantastic insistence on symmetry, serial repetition, and logical balance in the geometrical patterns and reliefs is justified. As most of the architectural structure or engineering is basically traditional in nature, the ornamentation tended to engulf or encrust the building (Holland Plaza, fig. 81; 120 Wall Street, fig. 82). There is a similarity in this case with the Gothic use of religious ornamentation, which in its abundance and iconography conveyed the idea of God. The Deco ornamentation had a similar function: to enhance or proselytize the idea of modernity. Consequently, the insistently flamboyant aspect of Deco ornamentation had a double import: on the one hand, to show the strength (banks), solidity (warehouse-factories), and hope (skyscrapers) of a disillusioned economic period and, on the other hand, to make symbolically manifest the nature of a new imagination of speed (travel), communications (radio), energy (electricity), and finally science (power).

Fig. 62   Salvation Army Building

Fig. 63   Sofia Warehouse

Fig. 64   261 Fifth Avenue

Fig. 65   Film Center

Fig. 66   Brooklyn Bank

Fig. 67   Wall Street Clock

Fig. 68   Church of the Heavenly Rest

Fig. 69   Staircase, Barbizon-Plaza Hotel

Fig. 70   Chrysler Building

Fig. 71   Staircase, Chrysler Building

Fig. 72   RKO Coloseum, 181st Street and Broadway

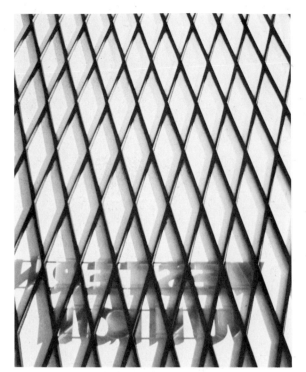

Fig. 73   Western Union Building

Fig. 74   210 East 68th Street

Fig. 75   Gracie Square

Fig. 76   22d Street and Second Avenue

Fig. 77   Barbizon-Plaza Hotel

Fig. 78   Health Building

Fig. 79   Chanin Building

Fig. 80 Irving Trust Building

Fig. 81   Holland Plaza

Fig. 82   120 Wall Street

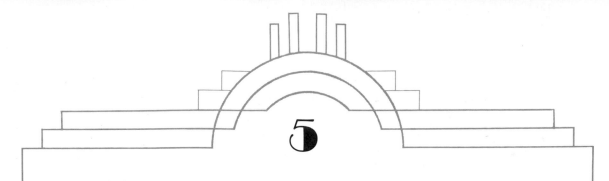

5

ARCHITECTURAL STYLISTIC DEVICES

SIMPLE STRUCTURE

As stated earlier, there were no complex structural or engineering problems involved with Deco architecture. This may be an oversimplification, especially where very tall skyscrapers are concerned. The problems of wind stress, weight loads, and so forth were unprecedented at such heights. They were calculable on a mathematical basis, however, which was in keeping with the scientific investigative aura of the time. Steel-cage construction, the zoning law pertaining to the stepback, high-speed elevators, and the slender tower format had already been determined by the early 1920s. Individual differences in detailing and minor fluctuations in number of stories, setbacks, area covered, and general conformation were determined by economics and budgets, not structural innovation.

Certain architectural stylistic devices, in one form or another, are found in almost all Deco buildings. These devices are formal ones, often incorporating Deco ornamentation but at times simply defining a particular detail or pointing to a specific effect.

The first of these devices was the ziggurat. So much has been said about this form already that it would be redundant to discuss it again at great length, although most of the previous material in this book dealt basically with form as a two-dimensional decorative device. It cannot be overemphasized that the ziggurat is the preeminently Deco structural form as well as the ornamental one (courthouse, fig. 83).

Window treatment plays an important role in Deco structure. The corner window presents a new architectural form with clarity. Inasmuch as the steel-cage con-

Fig. 83 Courthouse

struction allows the façade enormous flexibility in patterning, the corner, formerly load-bearing, could now be opened and cut in (Riverside Museum, fig. 84; Lexington and 57th Street, fig. 85; Majestic Apartments, fig. 86). Furthermore, the window could continue across the entire width of its expanse, creating the so-called ribbon window. On a more prosaic level, yet still concerned with an overall structural concept rather than an applied decorative one, is the use of the rounded corner window. This device would speed the transition of right-angle planes and give the building a more contained volumetric surface, especially when combined with the continuity of the ribbon window. Here a debt is owed to Mendelsohn's early work, the Schocken Department Store at Stuttgart.

Although post-Second World War, one of the most important versions of the ziggurat with curved corners is the Look Building (fig. 87).

This design conceit was not used extensively because of cost factors. Bending glass, even on a mass-produced basis, is expensive. An alternative solution is to chamfer the corner (83d Street and Madison Avenue, fig. 88) or to make the bend with a series of short connected planes (from two as in the Village Apartments, fig. 89, to three as in Bronx 2, fig. 90, and the El Dorado Apartments, fig. 91, to six as in the Rockefeller Apartments, fig. 92) which, however primitive, approximate enough of an arc to soften the turn. This faceting in conjunction with curved brickwork can be elegant. When the size of the building is massive

78

Fig. 84   Riverside Museum

(Starrett-Lehigh Building, fig. 93), the curving ribbon window can constrain its weight the way strapping does a bale of cotton.

The small pane of the so-called industrial window was used in the most expensive apartment houses (Tower Apartments, fig. 94) as well as in the warehouse-office block. The psychological connection with a technological innovation originally used in total glass expanses such as the Dessau Bauhaus (1925) must have been appealing for domestic use. This is an excellent example of the conversion of a structural device into an ornamental one.

Small useless balconies or terraces are used frequently in apartment houses to add a note of affluence or to vary the façade (West End Avenue, fig. 95; Madison Avenue and 88th Street, fig. 96). The rounded corners of the balconies perhaps recalled the poop decks of ocean liners, whose streamlining cut wind resistance while moving. This technological idea of the best or fastest way to travel deter-

Fig. 85   Lexington Avenue and 57th Street

79

Fig. 86   Majestic Apartments

mined the shape of various vehicles including the automobile (Chrysler Airflow), the steamship (*Normandy*), dirigibles, and airplanes. These forms are found repeatedly as architectural devices, partly to indicate the connection with the Futurist notion of dynamism.

Another variation on the balcony theme is the very small flare-up of the termination of a column (310 East 55th Street, fig. 2). This seems to be a reference to a medieval fortress (Women's House of Detention, fig. 1) or simply a capping at roof line. With Bloomingdale's this little bulge becomes a three-dimensional reverse ziggurat.

When the windows run in vertical strips the spandrels separating the floors are sometimes of a dark material or have heavy bas-relief. This color and/or texture visually combine with the glass so that the strip seems to run without interruption to the apex. Frequently, the capping of this strip is with a Deco ornament. At times the adjacent vertical pier has the same ornament or it has one and the window strip does not (Rockefeller Center, fig. 97; Squibb Building, fig. 98). The verticality of the buildings is increased enormously by leaving the roof line corniceless and open-ended. A sense of exciting expectation exists since there is the unconscious sense that the building could still include an unlimited number of additional stories rising endlessly into the clouds.

The crenelations found in many low-rise store buildings have a unique and fortresslike outline (store at Sheridan Square, fig. 99). These outcroppings are usually the terminations of columns in a ziggurat capital or the tips of floral bouquets (ZumZum, fig. 100). They present an urban skyline in miniature.

Such structural devices are used in direct relationship with ornamental devices and contribute to the integration of the architecture.

Fig. 87   Look Building

Fig. 88   83rd Street and Madison Avenue

Fig. 89   Village Apartments

Fig. 90   Bronx 2

Fig. 91   El Dorado Apartments

Fig. 92   Rockefeller Apartments

Fig. 94   Tower Apartments

Fig. 93   Starrett-Lehigh Building

Fig. 95   West End Avenue

Fig. 96   Madison Avenue and 88th Street

Fig. 97 Rockefeller Center

Fig. 98   Squibb Building

Fig. 99   Store at Sheridan Square

Fig. 100   Zum Zum

Two main types of Deco structure are found in New York City. Because the land values are high and space condensed, especially in Manhattan, buildings are packed together as closely as possible. Buildings usually are enclosed on three sides. It is rare when one is free on two or three sides, and freestanding structures are almost always those which occupy an entire block.

When the façade of the building is even with the lot line, it can rise only so far until it must recede and rise again as a separated but connected shaft. This shaft or tower can be thought of as freestanding, although the base from which it springs is surrounded completely up to a certain height.

The two types of structure then are those in the round and those which are basically façades.

Because façade-type buildings are closely packed, it is difficult, if not impossible, to see the entire building from any distance. There are actually only two ways to see these buildings fairly close up: at street level and from various heights of adjacent tall buildings.

Many Deco high-rise buildings (taking into consideration these visual distance limitations) concentrated Deco ornamentation at street level and at the roof line. The space between is generally devoid of decoration. This aspect of the Deco style is again related to the concept of

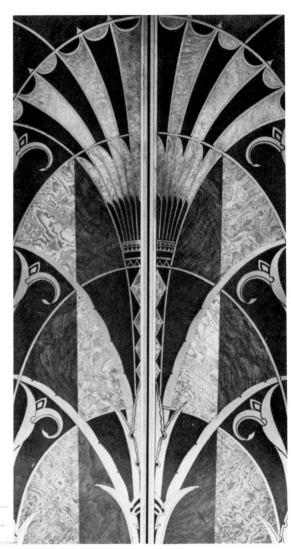

Fig. 101   Chrysler Building elevator

89

Fig. 102 Swiss Center Building elevator

the Deco building as a theatrical set, a dazzling entranceway; even the elevators are opulent (Chrysler Building, fig. 101; Swiss Center Building, fig. 102; Irving Trust Building, fig. 103). The beginning and the end of the day are started and finished with extreme style. The roof line is interesting and encrusted with ornamentation to make a kind of topping which relates to the decoration at street level. Thus there is a continuity of design which holds an individual building in place vertically.

But at ground level the façades are similar, and at the skyline the buildings merge and interrelate as a common, single outline, as varied and yet as closely knit as a range of great mountains.

Fig. 103   Irving Trust Building elevator

6

MATERIALS AND BUILDING FUNCTIONS

MATERIALS

The materials of Art Deco were the traditional marble, stone and brick, wood, bronze, and brass. The actual superstructure was steel, but the facings, interiors, and details contained every existing common material and, just as frequently, many exotic ones as well.

The fact that the structures themselves were not radically innovative made the use of known and tried materials interact in a related context. But, just as the ornamentation was modernistic, the materials were not used in traditional ways either. The juxtapositions of color, texture, pattern, and opulence often startled and even shocked. Not only was the rhythm of a shape jolting, but the material itself added an additional impact. Especially in interiors, where there is no weather problem, the theatrical effect could be rampant through the combined use of light, reflection, color, and absorption.

It was, to a large degree, an architecture of surfaces: shimmering, sparkling, dazzling, and active. There are no quiet places. The closest natural analogy would be the color and light of the Grand Canyon.

A number of new materials were invented in the early 1920s. Plastic was the main harbinger of the new technological potential, but at the time it had no structural strength and could not be used for a building's exterior ornamentation because it was not weather-resistant. It was, consequently, relegated for use in inexpensive *objets d'art* and jewelry.

Clear plastic or plexiglass had a more limited use, but it did have the advantage of conducting light through itself, and producing illumination from its edges (Swiss Center Building, elevator, fig. 104).

Glass brick was also acclaimed when first invented. It is a process of casting glass in a hollow translucent or textured cube or rectangle. Like plastic, this strange material had little structural strength. It did have a certain insulating property (trapped air space) and, of course, was transparent, though distorting, and translucent. Again, the glass brick had appeal because of its theatrical effect (1500 Grand Concourse, fig. 105). A wall of glass brick admitted light which was diffused and refracted. Images were broken into segments and abstracted as in a kaleidoscope. It was an exciting method of seeing on a relatively large scale. From the exterior, the sun reflected off of the blocks like a pile of crystals (83d Street and Madison Avenue, fig. 88; Porters', fig. 37).

Glass cast in a thin sheet of molded pattern is used even more infrequently than glass brick because of its enormous cost. The best example is a fantastically successful use of this material as a light modulated Futurist design at 30 Rockefeller Plaza (figs. 106, 107).

Neon light was an invention of the time, but it was hardly exploited in Deco building, although its potential as a design element seems to have been enormous. It is used in the lobby of the Chrysler Building (fig. 108), yet the tubes are hidden behind the ziggurat baffles. It was to graphics and advertising that the neon tube was relegated, primarily because its flexibility lent itself to that direction. The flashing, strobic, polychromed brilliance of Times Square was in its glory in the 1920s (there is the afterimage effect of the lightning flash as well), another indication of the surface quality of this Deco material. This pulsating collage of neon light relates to movement, speed, and Futurist technique and Cubist subject matter—that is, using graphic devices.

Stainless steel would have been *the* architectural Deco material: structural strength, mirrorlike reflectiveness, and the hard, bright, fast quality of streamlining. But it was economically unfeasible. It was, on rare occasions, used for ornamental trim (West End Avenue, fig. 95; Chrysler Building eagles or winged hats, fig. 109; General Electric Building mailbox, fig. 110; Chrysler Building information stand, fig. 108). It was aluminum, either polished (Chrysler Building spire, fig. 70) or pewter matte (Swiss Center ceiling, fig. 111), which replaced stainless steel. Relatively inexpensive, easily malleable or cast, aluminum could be used to cover large decorative expanses.

Returning to traditional materials, the richest and most prominent decorative material was marble. Some type is found in every skyscraper in the city; from the purest white Carrara (used most often in government buildings, Battery Highway Blockhouse, fig. 112) to the blackest of black Pyrenees (Rockefeller Center, fig. 113), or the extreme hard blackness of basalt (Bloomingdale's, fig. 114).

The descriptive or definitive materials or color combination, the *standard* of Deco thinking and ornamentation, are stainless steel and black marble. The perfectly mirror-reflective Yin coupled with polished

Fig. 104   Swiss Center Building elevator

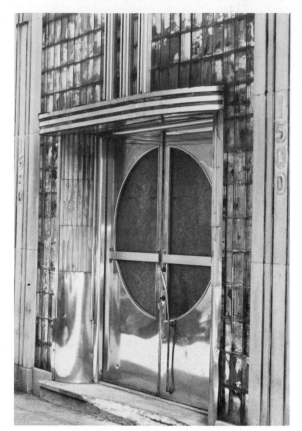

Fig. 105   1500 Grand Concourse

black absorptive Yang (Rockefeller Center escalator, fig. 115). This combination has the most elegant connotations. On a larger scale there was a stronger interest in highly colored and heavily patterned marbles (20 Broadway, fig. 116) and in some cases even in the expressive, wildly striated onyxes. Dark greens, reds and oranges, and browns, alone or in combination, were the more common variations.

The walls of the main floor of the Chrysler Building are rose flame marble and seem to encompass one in a fiery grotto (fig. 117). The sepia-flecked and red-veined cream Botticino of 60 Wall Street Tower (fig. 118) resembles the swirling eddies of antique end papers. The clean warm beige marble columns of 30 Rockefeller Plaza (fig. 107) have an imposing dignity.

Two traditional metals frequently used for bas-relief are bronze and brass. If used on the exterior, the reliefs are oxidized to a dark green or black patina. A high mirror polish is used on interior details (Rockefeller Center balustrade, fig. 119; Chanin Building balustrade and grates, fig. 79).

Fig. 106   30 Rockefeller Plaza

Fig. 108 Chrysler Building

Fig. 107 30 Rockefeller Plaza

Fig. 109   Chrysler Building

Fig. 110   General Electric Building mailbox

Fig. 111   Swiss Center ceiling

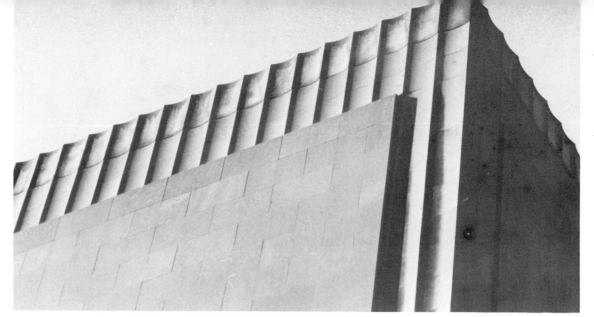

Fig. 112   Battery Highway Blockhouse

Fig. 113   Rockefeller Center

Fig. 114   Bloomingdale's

Fig. 115   Rockefeller Center escalator

Fig. 116   20 Broadway

Fig. 117   Chrysler Building

Fig. 118   60 Wall Street Tower

Fig. 119   Rockefeller Center balustrade

When wood is needed as a decorative element, it is always of the rare and expensive variety. Mahoganies, ebonies, teaks, burled maples and elms, koa wood, walnut, acacia, ironwood, and numerous fruitwoods are used in every possible combination (Chrysler Building elevator doors, fig. 120). The craft of marquetry was raised to a very high level.

Gold or silver leaf was seldom used because of the cost. The two major exceptions are the arched and corbeled ceilings of the General Electric Building (fig. 121) and the intricate linear patterns of the ceiling of the Bankers Trust (fig. 17a). Incidentally, Deco undergessoing was green instead of the classical red sienna. It imparted less brilliance but resembled aluminum.

Carved limestone was the usual material for elaborate decoration (431 East 52nd Street, fig. 122); denser stone such as gray granite was used also (church, 90th Street and Fifth Avenue, fig. 49).

Ironwork plays an important part in Deco ornamentation, because the design is, invariably, integrated with a necessary architectural detail: window grates (96th Street, fig. 123; Bell Telephone Building, fig. 124; Irving Trust Building, fig. 125, canopies (55 Central Park West, fig. 126), doors (1150 Grand Concourse, fig. 127), and gates (Baptist Church, 61st Street and Second Avenue, fig. 128). Wherever some type of protective screen or guard rail was needed, the welder could execute the wildest silhouette drawings of the designer. Geometric or floral, in the best

instances (Madison Avenue and 34th Street, fig. 129), the ironwork blended well with the entire building decoration (S. R. Guggenheim Museum, fig. 27). The ironwork railings on the overpass at the beginning of the Battery Highway are extraordinary (fig. 130). The only Deco subway entrance again exemplifies the skill and craftsmanship involved in this minor art when integrated with sophistication (fig. 131).

Decorative glass was either crystal and used in conjunction with metals, blue glass (China Inn, fig. 132), frosted glass, or mirror glass, which was faceted and curved around corners (Radio City, lounge, fig. 133) or attached in long vertical strips against an undulating surface (Barbizon-Plaza Hotel, fig. 134). Where frosted glass is concerned, great care and skill is necessary to avoid engraving too deeply and weakening the strength of the pane.

The resultant translucent and clear combination was a favorite Deco comparison. The soft, hazy surface was suitable for the filtering of light and was used in light fixtures (Majestic Apartments, fig. 135; Chrysler Building, fig. 136; Waldorf Astoria Hotel, fig. 137). Frosted glass permitted privacy without loss of light, and this type of screen function became fairly popular.

Blue mirrored glass was strictly an eccentric and infrequent decoration. As exterior units, mirrors interfered with any sense of solidity and were seen only on small store fronts, bars, or restaurants.

105

Fig. 120   Chrysler Building elevator

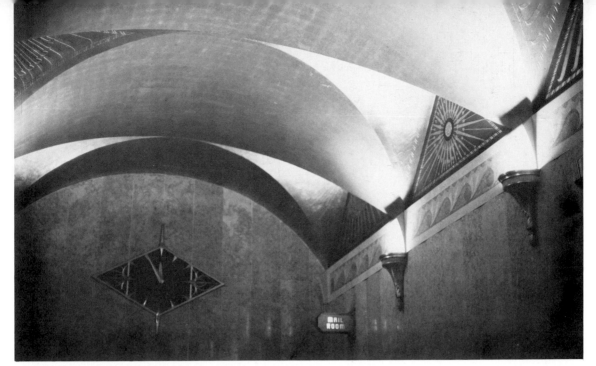

Fig. 121   General Electric Building

Fig. 122   431 East 52nd Street

Fig. 123   West 96th Street

Fig. 124   Bell Telephone Building

Fig. 125   Irving Trust Building

Fig. 126   55 Central Park West

Fig. 127   1150 Grand Concourse

Fig. 128   Baptist Church, 61st Street
            and Second Avenue

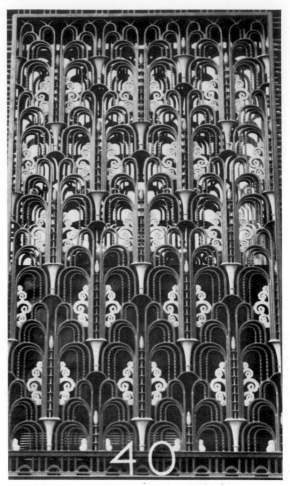

Fig. 129   Madison Avenue and 34th Street

Fig. 130　Battery Highway overpass

Fig. 132　China Inn

Fig. 131　Subway Entrance

Fig. 133　Radio City lounge

Fig. 134   Barbizon-Plaza Hotel

Fig. 135 Majestic Apartments

Fig. 136   Chrysler Building

Mosaics are found usually, along with blue glass, in rather flashy interiors such as Garfield's Cafeteria in Brooklyn. Often mosaics are the only small colored notes in otherwise dull bricked façades (Passy Restaurant, fig. 138). In the Irving Trust Building's reception hall (fig. 139), however, the modern use of mosaic reached heights reminiscent of Ravenna or the glories of the Byzantine ceiling. In a space 37 feet high there are 8,911 square feet of Venetian glass mosaics, two thousand of which are gold and the balance composed of reds and oranges, the most costly of all mosaic colors. The design of the room, as well as that of the mosaics, was worked out by the architects, but actually detailed by Hildreth Meiers (fig. 140). The patterns are abstract yet have the crackling energy of lightning and movement. The integration of bronze details and bas-reliefs, red Verona marble columns (fig. 141), mosaic, and lightning make this, along with the lobby of the Chrysler Building and Radio City Music Hall, one of the great Deco spaces in the city.

Ceramic tiles were one way to introduce color to the exterior of a building. Generally, it was used with restraint and as an accent. The water tank enclosure of the Tower Apartments on 38th Street (fig. 94) runs an undulating rainbow around its periphery.

Sometimes the combinations of color are harsh and blatant, covering the entire three or four stories of a building (200 Park Avenue, fig. 8). At other times they are in a harmonious blend of analogous hues, as in 261 Fifth Avenue (fig. 64) or 29th Street and Park Avenue South, where the blues range from cobalt to light cerulean blue. Green and black tiles are an important part of the entrance doors and third-story frieze of two apartment houses (210 East 68th Street, fig. 74; 22d Street and Second Avenue, fig. 76).

Brick was *the* basic exterior material for the more plebeian buildings, including smaller apartment blocks, warehouse-offices, low stores, docks, and factories-offices. Tonal or textural varieties were used for Deco patterns through the intricate, creative laying of courses (Daily News Building, fig. 142; 320 Central Park West, fig. 143). In some way or another, the bricklayer added his touch of modernity by including a fillip of geometric Deco pattern (Grand Concourse, fig. 144; Western Union Building, fig. 145).

Fig. 138 Passy Restaurant

Fig. 137 Waldorf Astoria Hotel

Fig. 139   Irving Trust Building

Fig. 140   Irving Trust Building

Fig. 141   Irving Trust Building

BUILDING FUNCTIONS

Deco architecture was not limited to any one particular kind of building. The style affected all aspects of life, and thus the functions of work, travel, housing, entertainment, shopping, religion, education, health, and incarceration were the subject matter of the architecture, as they were in the past.

The following are the principal building types found in the New York environment:

WORK	HIGH-RISE OFFICE BUILDINGS Skyscrapers Medium Height
	OFFICE-FACTORY-WAREHOUSE BLOCKS, LOW-RISE STORES
LIVING	APARTMENT HOUSES High-rise Low blocks Housing Developments Hotels

SERVICES	HOSPITALS, SCHOOLS, PRISONS, BANKS, GOVERNMENTAL, GARAGES, RELIGIOUS
SHOPPING AND ENTERTAINMENT	DEPARTMENT STORES, THEATERS, SMALL SHOPS, RESTAURANTS
TRAVEL	PIERS, HIGHWAYS, BRIDGES, TUNNELS

Skyscrapers

The one major change in building style had to do with work. White-collar business, law, and corporate headquarters (especially banking and finance) occupied the type of building which most typifies the style: the skyscraper.

The economic situation—the traumatic shift from prosperity to depression—seemed to nurture the dreamlike hope (height equals aspiration) in reaching upward, as coincidentally the movie palace had the function of fantasy catharsis. Many of the great skyscrapers were planned or begun in the latter part of the 1920s and finished in the early 1930s. Included in this group are the following buildings: Empire State, Chrysler, 111 John Street, Daily News, 21 Broadway, 60 Wall Street Tower, General Electric, and McGraw-Hill.

In terms of the lavish details and appointments involved in construction, there was apparently no cutback or reduction because of the stock market crash. The drop in labor and material costs and the ready availability of master craftsmen more than compensated for any material or design specification expense incurred originally.

Earlier, 1900–1915, the plan for the

high-rise office building gradually developed a standard street-level base of some ten to twenty stories at lot line, from which sprang a slender rectangular shaft, usually capped with one of the fashionable neorevivals: Gothic, Roman, and so on (the Singer Building by Ernest Flagg, 1908, and the Woolworth Building by Cass Gilbert, 1913). There were exceptions to this formula. Actually a great many buildings rose in a massive surge directly from lot line to their full height. The Flatiron Building by D. H. Burnham, 1902, and primarily the Equitable Building by Ernest R. Graham, 1915, condensed an extreme amount of floor space in relation to the actual site area.

This compacting presaged the 1916 zoning law and later the 1923 setback law, which was to determine the future form of the high-rise building. After the Second World War the slab shape made its appearance (Lever House, 1952, S.O.M.; U.N. Building, 1947–1953, Wallace K. Harrison, and so on), with plazas and open spaces at ground level. This type of structure became the formula for hundreds of glass-skinned office buildings found throughout the world, from Park Avenue (which Nervi dubbed "Una Strada Superba") to Japan. The most current form of skyscraper is the load-bearing wall tower or slab. Eero Saarinen with his C.B.S. Building of 1965 built one of the first high-rise skyscrapers employing load-bearing wall principles. (Incidentally Eliel Saarinen, Eero's father, was a Deco architect of refined sensitivity and nuance. Cranbrook and Kingswood schools in Bloomfield, Michigan, remain fine examples in their own right.) The new McGraw-Hill Building and the World Trade Center are other load-bearing wall structures.

The general form of the Deco skyscraper developed during the 1920s but reached its culmination in 1932–1937. Many Deco towers were crowned with some graduated geometric conformation terminating in a pointed protuberance, which in some cases was functional broadcasting antennae. At one time the Empire State pinnacle was considered as a dirigible mooring mast. In Chicago the Palmolive Building mast houses a revolving beacon. In a design sense this manner of finishing related to the idea of a spire which was spiritually symbolic. It also had the primitive symbolism of a spear or lance thrust or scraping the sky. There was an obvious phallic connotation. Other versions of the pinnacle conformation involved variations of ziggurat forms carried to an extreme end in a narrow shaft; or, as in the case of the General Electric Building (fig. 146), and the Barbizon-Plaza (fig. 147), recall motifs of the ray-gun fantasies of science fiction.

A great deal of effort and expense was spent on interiors and detail decoration, particularly in lobbies and with elevators. The full gamut of Deco devices—the motifs, the materials, the lighting—went into a well-integrated composite, often opulently self-indulgent. If the architect was limited in his spacial articulation of the building as a total form, he could leap artistically overboard into the ornamentation. What form there was, was distorted by emphasis and stylized into a chic modernism.

Fig. 142   Daily News Building

Fig. 144   Grand Concourse

Fig. 143   320 Central Park West

Fig. 145   Western Union Building

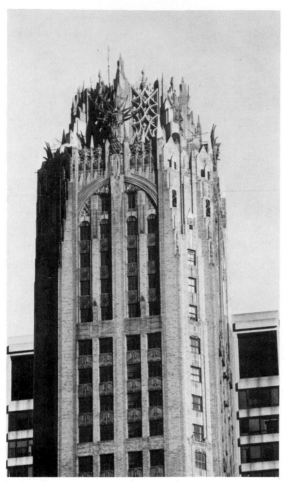

Fig. 146 General Electric Building

Fig. 147 Barbizon-Plaza Hotel

Office-Factory-Warehouse Blocks

Another type particularly suited to the application of Deco thinking was the massive office-factory-warehouse complex. The structure was quite straightforward and functional—perhaps the most direct sense of certain Corbusian principles. Historically the early American factory scheme was one of the structures which impressed Le Corbusier when he visited the United States. This unadorned and truly functional building (a circular Shaker cow barn, for instance) inspired the often misunderstood maxim "a machine for living." Simple, open, column-bearing horizontal floors, with skins of concrete or brick and large industrial windows, were the formula for the Deco factory block. In-evitably Deco ornamentation, always geometric unless of a governmental type, wound its way throughout the façade and in the poorest building was achieved by patterning the brick courses (Western Union Building, fig. 145). Because of the sheer mass of some of the buildings, continuous horizontal windows, either ribbon or with narrowly placed mullions, kept the structure earthbound (Starrett-Lehigh Building, fig. 93). Although there was more honest thinking involved in defining the floors and a greater concern with the sequences of the stepbacked terraces, there is still the impression of an *objet d'art* giganticized rather than a monumental structure.

Low-Rise Stores

Deco ornamentation is found on all types of building, but it takes on an eccentric twist in the two- or three-story storefront block. Since the roof line is easily visible, the outline of the cornice is cut in or otherwise crenelated (Sheridan Square, fig. 99; Kress, fig. 148). Interspersed between pseudocapitals or piers is either floral decoration (Eighth Avenue, fig. 149; ZumZum, fig. 100) or some other type. In the case of Kress, the decoration is a mimicking of Mayan glyphs.

Apartment Houses

The high-rise apartment house, twenty to thirty stories, emulated, with an equally if not more luxurious finish, the office lobby (888 Grand Concourse, fig. 150). Actually the apartment building and especially the hotel were stylistically interchangeable with the office building. It takes little stretch of the imagination to convert the lobby of the Swiss Center or 60 Wall Street Tower into an apartment house foyer; and conversely the lobby of the Barbizon-Plaza, stripped of its rugs and chandelier, could easily be an efficient business headquarters.

Many other, smaller apartment buildings were constructed at this time, including large federally sponsored housing developments or blocks (Hillman Houses, fig. 151). The tower conformation was not used, however, and the plans generally were similar to the simple massive block of the warehouse. Again nothing was attempted in the way of structural innovation. The window treatment emphasized horizontality; and the external decoration was usually limited to fancy geometric brickwork geared to the ribbon or corner turns of the windows.

Fig. 148   Kress

Fig. 149   Eighth Avenue

Fig. 150   888 Grand Concourse

Fig. 151   Hillman Houses

Fig. 152   New York Hospital

Fig. 153   New York Hospital

New York Hospital was originally finished in 1933, but later additions and extensions have not altered its Cubist massing. Simple pointed arch windows have a unifying effect overall (fig. 152). Details are Spartan (fig. 153), and like other enormous Deco blocks, the size and density determine the style rather than the ornamentation. This is also the case with Columbia-Presbyterian Medical Center, 1928, although the site is high above the Hudson River (Bard Hall, fig. 154). Memorial Sloan-Kettering Cancer Center, 1935, is a smaller yet imposing structure, and the addition to St. Vincent's, 1935, includes some primitive Deco bas-reliefs in an otherwise undistinguished façade. The small private hospital Le Roy at 40 East 61st Street has the same facing as the apartment house on 85th and Madison Avenue but with different and fine medical-snake ironwork doors (fig. 155).

Two important Deco colleges are Hunter, 1940, and the New School for Social Research, 1930. Neither school has geometric or floral embellishment. Instead, one favors the strong horizontal and textural statement of Expressionism and the other is similar to the industrial factory. In both cases, interest is focused in the fenestration, and the spacing of the windowpanes sets up a powerful rhythmic direction (Hunter College, fig. 156). At The New School, the device of gradually angling the façade (actually the cantilevered floors) inward toward the upper stories is as subtle and effective as entasis is in a Greek column (fig. 157).

The Women's House of Detention has been covered in detail in the Preface. Other Deco prisons include the Tombs, which is part of the Criminal Courts Building, 1939, a classical Deco ziggurat (fig. 83). The Men's Detention Building on West Street and 11th Street, 1938, is a simple five-story structure with large translucent industrial windows. From a security viewpoint this type of small pane (if the metal framing is strong enough and fixed) affords the advantage of increasing the light source without the added precautionary need for screening or bars.

Governmental buildings include those involved with various bureaucratic and federal functions. The Criminal Courts Building already mentioned above, the United States Courthouse (which was designed by one of the two men who engineered the George Washington Bridge, Cass Gilbert), the State Building, and the Health Building across the street are a few of the types which are prevalent. Large, gray limestone or white marble, restrained but muscular, are apt descriptions of this phase of Deco classicism. Another excellent example is the Federal Post Office on Church Street. Banks might just as well fall under this category. Most were located on the ground floor of high-rise buildings (fig. 158), but many were freestanding edifices (Provident Loan Society, fig. 159). Stolid, imposing, and fortresslike, banks needed to rein-

127

force the image of security during a time when even a dime was precious.

Churches and temples proliferated in the latter half of the 1920s. In fact most of the synagogues in Manhattan were built between 1926 and 1929. They were largely Moorish or Near Eastern in design. Occasionally there would be some Deco geometric bas-relief underlying the intricacies of the Alhambra arabesques.

And perched atop the columns of Temple Emanu-El are two splendid mechanistic robot lions (fig. 46). Churches fluctuated between the straight Romanesque additions of St. Bartholomew's, 1919 and 1927, to the reworking of the Gothic in the Deco manner, as in the Church of the Heavenly Rest, 1928 (fig. 49). The one studied and bizarre church which was unabashedly unafraid of its convictions is Trinity Baptist, 1930, by Martin Hedmark (fig. 160), a transitional church whose architect could not evade his Deco element yet struggled for the tenderness of the Art Nouveau.

Either the architects of religious buildings felt restricted in regard to modernistic style because of the conservative nature of the subject matter or they felt they had to design in a more traditional stylistic mode—choosing whichever previous century suited the congregation. Whatever the reason, there is no Deco religious building of distinction.

Fig. 154   Bard Hall

Fig. 155   Le Roy Hospital

Fig. 156   Hunter College

Fig. 157   The New School

Fig. 158   Manufacturers Hanover Trust

Fig. 159   Provident Loan Society

Fig. 160   Trinity Baptist Church

Department Stores, Theaters, Small Shops, Restaurants

The elegant department store and small shop design flourished during the 1930s. (There is nothing in New York that has the strength of Carson, Pirie and Scott in Chicago by Sullivan or Schocken in Germany by Mendelsohn.) In contrast Bloomingdale's (fig. 114) and Bonwit's (but not Tiffany's, which *is* a clearer statement) tend to be thin and concerned with surface. The Deco style here becomes snobbish and flowery. It is a far cry from the movie palace (but not Radio City Music Hall), whose effects are crass, dramatic, and exaggerated. The department store and small shop (plants, fig. 161; drugstore, fig. 162; Lipkind Shoes, fig. 163) chose to sheath their form in an elegant and sophisticated, often restrained façade which reflected the quality of their merchandise. The Art Deco style in this genre was a truly integrated one. It met the needs of its consumers both economically and spiritually. It was almost pure fashion, from the lowest (fad) to the highest (class).

With sound films the movie theater quickly became an inexpensive haven for the general public. It was a place to escape to, to forget reality, to dream (theaters were often called "dream palaces"). Their names were exotic, and one went to them as if on a voyage or excursion. The movies became quickly one of the most important mass entertainments in history (second at the time only to the radio). The films needed suitable auditoriums to match and house their fantastic imagery. Until the early thirties the Deco design of movie theaters was extremely eclectic, drawing from the Moorish (Harlem, fig. 164), Byzantine, and Gothic (not unlike religious buildings) directly. But by the middle thirties the otherworldly or futuristic flavor of Deco (itself influenced by esoteric archetypes) gained predominance and probably reached its apex of sophistication and streamlining in Radio City Music Hall (figs. 165, 166). Moreover, by this time the Deco style was being used in its most exaggerated and full-blown sense in movie sets, props, and furniture. The platinum blonde on the silver screen would have been exactly in her milieu in the actual lobby.

Restaurants, like the small shop, constantly changed their décor. By the post-world war era, practically every Deco restaurant had been remodeled. A notable exception is the Rainbow Room of Rockefeller Center, whose crystal railing and balustrade supports are as elegantly stylish as the later chandeliers are out of keeping. The interior of the Restaurant Passy is designed in the rarefied French manner and is still completely intact. One of the most consistent promoters (along with the New York Telephone Company, which has six major Deco buildings) of the style was the Horn and Hardart restaurant chain. Each of its branches was Deco-inspired. The one on 181th Street (fig. 167) is spectacular. Another interesting exterior is the China Inn, which exploits blue mirrored glass in a vertical ziggurat motif about its entranceway. Finally the Munson Diner is a unique type fashioned like an aerodynamic train car. This form of eatery began during the

1920s as a small roadside food stop for truckers and travelers. The Munson Diner is an original modular prototype, and the design is still being produced today.

Because the automobile came into widespread use during the 1920s, by the end of the decade the city had dozens of public garages. Most of them were built between 1925 and 1930 and ranged from huge and elaborate structures (City Garage, fig. 168) to medium size ones, housing fifty to a hundred cars. One (45th Street and First Avenue, fig. 169) has the simplicity and honesty to reveal its ramp structure in the exterior elevation, making the entire building a zigzag pattern.

Fig. 161   Small shop

Fig. 162   Drugstore

132

Fig. 163   Lipkind Shoes

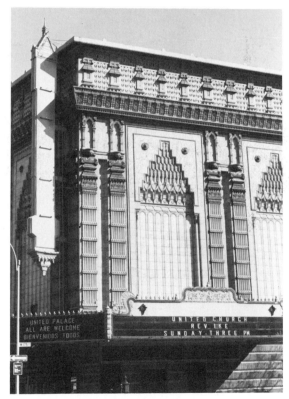

Fig. 164   Movie Theater, Harlem

Fig. 165   Radio City Music Hall

Fig. 166   Radio City Music Hall

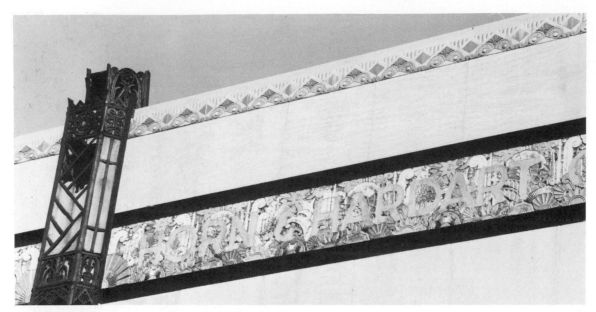

Fig. 167   Horn and Hardart

Fig. 168   City Garage

Fig. 169   Garage, 45th Street and First Avenue

Fig. 170   West Side Highway

Fig. 171   West Side Highway

Fig. 172   Riverside Park

While the buildings were climbing vertically at a rapid rate, the arteries of transportation were keeping equal pace. New highways and various entrances and crossroads into the city were necessary to keep the logistical flow of supplies and people constant and moving. The elevated West Side Highway (fig. 170) was an eminently functional structure which left little room or expense for ornamentation. This did not deter the designers, who ingeniously utilized Deco patterns in the ironwork and especially in the riveting. The winged wheel, a winged hourglass, an ominous double-winged hooded set of cogwheels, plus the ever-present guardian eagles (fig. 171) compose the high bas-relief escutcheon embossed every four or five blocks along the side of the highway. The railings for the approaches to the highway from Riverside Park (fig. 172) have elegant ironwork supports which relate more to a Nouveau silhouette (a direct steal from A. H. Mackmurdo) than Deco. The ramps from West Street onto the highway begin or end with a carved stone wheellike flower (fig. 173).

The Holland Tunnel, named after C. F. Holland, the architect-engineer who designed it, was finished in 1927. The Queens-Midtown Tunnel was completed in 1940. The core of the Lincoln Tunnel was finished in 1937. The blockhouses and twin spotlight towers at the entranceway (from the New York side) are contrasts in massive solidity with open steel structure (fig. 174). The earlier light towers (fig. 175) are almost exact copies of the portal lights outside the State Building on Court Street (fig. 176).

There were some dockside façades which followed the standard construction for piers done in the 1930s. Interest is mainly centered in the geometric working of the glazed brickwork.

Of the sixty bridges constructed in New York City since 1900, only sixteen were finished prior to 1920 and only fifteen since 1940. Twenty-nine bridges were completed between 1920 and 1940, including the Triborough, 1936; Bronx-Whitestone, 1939; Henry Hudson, 1936; Bayonne, 1931; and George Washington, 1931. All five of these span more than 1,000 feet and range from suspension to arched to truss types. The longest (at least until 1937) at 3,500 feet and incredibly breathtaking is the George Washington. It was finished in the same year as the Empire State Building, and the city had the distinction of having the longest horizontal and highest vertical structures in the world. This element of power—that is, having the physical most of something—was consonant with a fantasy image made real and a Deco design program which implied that more is better, even though economically the city was suffering.

Fig. 173   West Street ramps

Fig. 174   Lincoln Tunnel

Fig. 175   Lincoln Tunnel

Fig. 176   State Building, Court Street

7

CONCLUSION: GOTHIC SIMILARITIES AND ARCHITECTURAL ANONYMITY

Elayne Varian has implied that the Deco period was the last era in modern building in which industrial crafts and quality workmanship were integrated with the concepts of the architect, in which stonemasons, metalworkers, mosaicists, muralists, and sculptors were all of one mind, not only in regard to the interrelationship of the style but also in the fine precision and finish of their individual crafts.

This is true in the sociological sense of a feudal system of crafts delegation. In this way an analogy with the Gothic is justified. Economically there is a further similarity. Each skyscraper bears, along with its symbolic reference as a machine-age cathedral, the beehive center of the dedicated masses rebuilding a wounded economy. Faith, however, is transferred and channeled from an omnipotent God to an omnipotent machine power/ science. The intermediaries and consolidators are no longer kings and popes but Rockefellers, Chryslers, McGraw, and/or vaticanate corporations: Bell Telephone, Western Union, R.C.A., and General Electric. These entrepreneurs along with the government (Roosevelt elected in 1932) propagated the illusion of unity through architecture, economics, and politics until the Second World War. Beyond the sociological reasons for linking the Deco with the Gothic, there is a fundamental error in equating consensus design with craftsmanship quality. Usually on large-scale projects (cathedrals or skyscrapers) a consensus of intention is required to keep all the various design segments integrated. With both Deco and the Gothic the *style* itself was the unifying integer. This factor is not *necessarily* true. Individual creativity can be as powerful. The 1930s was not the last period of quality craftsmanship. It takes as much skill to construct the detail between the glass and mullion of the Seagram Building as it does to sculpt a radiator grille; and the even wash of light in the lobby of the same building surpasses any of the theatrical and dramatic effects of the lobby of the Chrysler building. The consummate skill involved with the mortise fitting of granite blocks of the Ford Foundation Building by Dinkeloo and Roche is more demanding than the floral frieze of the Chanin Building or the geometric brickwork of the Daily News Building two and three blocks away. The steel welding of Paul Rudolph's Black Townhouse on 63d Street is the ultimate statement of this difficult craft. The clearest example of post-Deco detailing and ornamentation is the welded I-beam vertical rails across the façade of the Seagram Building. Mies van der Rohe used this device originally on 860 Lake Shore Drive in Chicago in 1951. Because the supporting columns needed to be sheathed in concrete for fire-retarding reasons, Mies enclosed them in bronze sheeting. To the outside of those and the mullions are attached the I-beams which soar to the full height of the tower. They are pure decoration, aesthetically expressing the internal structure, externally.

The finesse and care, elegance and skill, of these details indicate that individual creative interpretation can be executed with as much fidelity as the best of Deco stylizations.

Deco architecture was an anonymous architecture. That is, like the Gothic, individual creative drive was subservient to and superseded by the force and strength of the style itself. The structural formula was relatively inflexible, and so was the ornamental one.

Every Deco architect or firm was able to design within the confines of the style, and they could emphasize the floral, the geometric, the more streamlined version of the middle thirties, or combinations of all three, with equal facility. Sloan and Robertson could be as relentlessly florid as they were in the Chanin Building (fig. 29), but then shift to the very cubic massiveness of 80 Broad Street (fig. 61). Schultz and Weaver not only did the florid 1657 Broadway and the Waldorf-Astoria Hotel but the Sherry-Netherland Hotel in 1927 and the Hotel Pierre in 1928 as well. Cross and Cross could reach from the Gothic geometricity of the General Electric Building (fig. 146) to the Deco classicism of 741 Fifth Avenue (fig. 177) and ultimately to the extremely floral City Bank at 65 Beaver Street. Buchanan and Kahn jumped from an encrusted geometric façade at 304 East 45th Street, 120 Wall Street, and 261 Fifth Avenue to the restrained classicism of the Squibb Building (fig. 98).

The most radical shift in manner was from the banal pseudomonumental unfinished Hearst Building (fig. 178) to the Expressionist streamlining of the New School for Social Research by Joseph Urban. Emery Roth could do something as Gothic in mood as 5 East 57th Street and as Venetian in texture as the Ardsley Apartments at 320 Central Park West (fig. 179).

Voorhees, Gmelin, and Walker had a definite straightforward and almost distinguishable style within the style. Their work for the N.Y. Telephone Company was consistently articulate and exploratory. The similarity between buildings with such diverse functions as the Salvation Army (fig. 62), Brooklyn Bank (fig. 66), and Bell at 210 West 18th Street is remarkable.

The factor of stylistic anonymity is further emphasized by the interchangeability of various architects with various firms. The amiable relationships between firms and partners was extraordinary. John Mead Howells, who did Beekman Towers, 1928 (fig. 32), alone, collaborated with Raymond Hood on the Daily News Building. Hood worked with J. Andre Fouilhoux and Harrison on Rockefeller Center, while Fouilhoux joined with Harrison on the Rockefeller Apartments on 54th Street (fig. 92) and Hunter College (fig. 156). Shreve, Lamb, and Harmon, architects of the Empire State, also collaborated with Harrison and Fouilhoux on Hunter. Kenneth Murchison joined Godley and Hood, again with Fouilhoux, to do the Beaux-Arts Apartments (fig. 180). Probably the greatest cooperative venture of the entire Deco period was on Rockefeller Center. The leading architects (or at least the team with first billing) was Reinhard and Hofmeister; then, Corbett, Harrison, and MacMurray; then Hood and Fouilhoux. Harvey Wiley Corbett had also done the

Metropolitan Life Insurance Company with D. Everett Waid and the vast federal complex, the Criminal Courthouse (fig. 83) downtown. Arthur Loomis Harmon alone did Shelton Towers in 1924, and Thomas Lamb alone did two high-rise apartment houses, one on East 96th Street (fig. 181) and one on West 96th Street (fig. 123). Both buildings used the same iron grillwork over the floor-level windows. While Sloan and Robertson are credited completely with the Chanin Building, Irwin S. Chanin and Jacques De La Marre were considerably involved in the design, especially the interior, and De La Marre designed the famous convector grilles. Chanin then went on to the Century Apartments, the Majestic Apartments, and Green Acres. His last large project was the high-rise office building of 1970 which replaced the old Metropolitan Opera House.

In 1922 Raymond Hood, in collaboration with John Mead Howells, won the Tribune Tower competition in Chicago. Their conservative Gothic entry outscored many superior and advanced proposals. While this solution was anachronistic, the tower at least had some grace compared to the American Radiator Building, 40 West 40th Street (fig. 182), which Hood designed in 1924—an overblown exercise in Deco cum Gothic with the grosser aspects of both predominant.

John Mead Howells meanwhile had built Beekman Towers Hotel, a simple and clear, if unassuming, soft Deco expression. When Howells and Hood joined in 1930 for the Daily News Building, there was little reason to expect a modern

Fig. 177   741 Fifth Avenue

Fig. 178   Hearst Building

Fig. 179   Ardsley Apartments, 320 Central Park West

Fig. 180   Beaux-Arts Apartments

Fig. 181   Apartment, East 96th Street

Fig. 182 American Radiator Building   Fig. 183 McGraw-Hill Building

structure. The assumption is that Hood absorbed the motivations and aesthetics from certain of his competitors in Chicago, any one of whom (Eliel Saarinen, Walter Gropius, Hans Scharoun) was better qualified to deal with modern ideas. After being further involved in the Rockefeller project, Hood was primed to take on the McGraw-Hill commission. Since Godley and Fouilhoux were partners, it is a moot point about how influential Hood was in regard to the total concept. James McGraw encouraged a radical design concept, but perhaps it was the unsung J. Andre Fouilhoux who provided it. It was Fouilhoux, again with Harrison, who designed the Trylon and Perisphere (fig. 184) for the New York World's Fair of 1939, probably the most famous single symbol of modernity of the entire era. In any case, the McGraw-Hill Building (fig. 183) was an eccentric yet fairly successful amalgam of Deco and International Style elements.

Art Deco architects, finally, remain in a limbo, part of the great wave of artists and artisans swept away in an anonymous undertow while the Deco spindrift remained.

During the same period, roughly twenty years, some of the greatest architecture of all times was created, centered for the most part in Europe. Never before had there been such a concentration of individual architectural genius: Mies van der Rohe, Le Corbusier, Alvar Aalto, Wright, Nervi, Mendelsohn, Gropius, Gerrit Rietveldt. Separate buildings spring to mind: the Barcelona Pavilion and the Tugendhat House; the Kaufmann House at Bear Run; the Villa Savoye and Villa Garches; Turun Sanormat in Finland; the Bauhaus itself; Orbitello Hangars, Italy. These names have been branded in history. But who remembers Ralph Walker, Chanin, Joseph Urban, Russel and Walter, Cory, Thomas Lamb, Arthur Harmon, or even William Van Alen?

In retrospect it is difficult to evaluate or even see the wealth of ornamental architecture in the New York environment. Practically every street has its surprises. In some of the midtown or downtown areas the almost organic proliferation of geometric carving seemingly grows like lichen across the skyline. The pointed shafts, the craft involved in a polished cast bronze doorway, the delight of a geometric eagle standing guard, the special quality of neon or fluorescence—all these aspects of Deco are so familiar as to be unseen.

It is a tribute to New York architecture that individually it is anonymous. What is pertinent aesthetically is the skyline itself: that irregular, yet rhythmic mass of energy, the brain-wave pattern of a vital and protean city.

Fig. 184   Trylon and Perisphere

8

STYLISTIC LISTING OF ART DECO BUILDINGS

OFFICE SKYSCRAPERS

MIDTOWN

1931	350 Fifth Avenue	Empire State	Shreve, Lamb, and Harmon
1931	330 West 42d Street	McGraw-Hill	Hood, Godley, and Fouilhoux
1931	570 Lexington Avenue	General Electric	Cross and Cross
1930	405 Lexington Avenue	Chrysler	William Van Alen
1929	122 East 42d Street	Chanin	Sloan and Robertson
1930	220 East 42d Street	Daily News	John Mead Howells and Hood
1931	West 48th to West 51st Streets	Rockefeller Center	Reinhard and Hofmeister Corbett, Harrison, and MacMurray Hood and Fouilhoux
1932	1 Madison Avenue	Metropolitan Life Insurance	Harvey Wiley Corbett and D. Everett Waid
1929	261 Fifth Avenue		Buchman and Kahn
1931	275 Madison Avenue	Johns-Manville	Kenneth Frangheim
1930	745 Fifth Avenue	Squibb Building	Buchman and Kahn
1929	185 Montague Street Brooklyn	American Bank and Trust Company	Corbett, Harrison, and MacMurray

1931	101 Willoughby Street	New York Telephone	Voorhees, Gmelin, and Walker
1929	41 East 57th Street	Fuller Building	Walker and Gillette
1930	3 East 57th Street	Plummer McCutcheon	Shreve, Lamb, and Harmon
1926	5 East 57th Street		Emery Roth
1928	957 Eighth Avenue	Hearst Building	Joseph Urban
1931	500 Fifth Avenue		Shreve, Lamb, and Harmon
1948	488 Madison Avenue	Look Building	Emery Roth and Sons
1932	49th Street and Fifth Avenue	Swiss Center	Roy C. Marris
1927	551 Fifth Avenue	Fred F. French Building	Fred F. French Company
1931	444 Madison Avenue	Newsweek Building	Robert D. Kohn
1928	1657 Broadway		Schultze and Weaver
1928	1776 Broadway	Lazarus Building	George and Edward Blum
1929	304 East 45th Street	Allied Arts Building	Buchman and Kahn
1930	259–265 West 14th Street		William Whitehall
1931	741 Fifth Avenue	Manufacturers Trust	Cross and Cross
1927	40 East 34th Street 181 Madison Avenue		Whitney, Warren, and Wetmore
1929	630 Ninth Avenue	Film Center Building	Buchman and Kahn

OFFICE SKYSCRAPERS

DOWNTOWN

1929	111 John Street		Buchman and Kahn
1932	1 Wall Street	Irving Trust	Voorhees, Gmelin, and Walker

1932	70 Pine Street	60 Wall Street Tower	Clinton and Russell
1931	29 Broadway		Sloan and Robertson
1926	18–21 West Street	Downtown Athletic Club	Starrett and Van Vleck
1930	Church Street	American Stock Exchange	Starrett and Van Vleck
1931	120 Wall Street		Buchman and Kahn
1931	99 Wall Street		Schwartz and Gross
1931	80 Broad Street	Maritime Exchange	Sloan and Robertson
1934	26 Cortlandt Street	East River Savings Bank	Walker and Gillette
1929	60 John Street		Clinton and Russell
1937	65 Beaver Street	City Bank Farmers Trust Company	Cross and Cross
1929	17th Street 18th Street	Bell Telephone	Voorhees, Gmelin, and Walker
1930	17 John Street		Clinton and Russell Holton and George
1929	40 Wall Street	Bank of the Manhattan Company	H. Craig Severance and Yasuo Matsui

OFFICE/WAREHOUSE/FACTORY BLOCK

1927	200 Park Avenue		Ely Jacques Kahn
1930	45 Columbus Avenue	Sofia Warehouse	Jardine, Hill, and Murdock
1931	26th to 27th Streets From Eleventh to Twelfth Avenues	Starrett-Lehigh	Russell and Walter Cory, Yasuo Matsui
1930	60 Hudson Street	Western Union	Voorhees, Gmelin, and Walker
1928	36 Sixth Avenue	Bell Telephone	Voorhees, Gmelin, and Walker
1929	120 West 14th Street	Salvation Army	Voorhees, Gmelin, and Walker
1912 1928–39	154–160 West 14th Street		Alfred Felheimer Isaac Allen

1928	1375 Broadway	Lefcourt State	Buchman and Kahn
1928	Greenwich Avenue and 13th Street	Con Ed Blockhouse	
1927	419 Park Avenue South		Walter Haesli
1931	435 West 50th Street	Bell Telephone	Voorhees, Gmelin, and Walker
1930	431 Canal Street	Holland Plaza Block	Buchman and Kahn
1928	Block Bordered by Eighth Avenue 15th and 16th Streets and Ninth Avenue	New York Port Authority	
1925	200 Lexington Avenue	Furniture Exchange	York and Sawyer Buchman and Kahn
1931	100 Sixth Avenue		Shampan and Shampan

LOW-RISE STORES

1930	100 East 42d Street	Airlines Building	John Sloan
1928	304 East 44th Street	Reeves Sound Studio	Dennison and Hirons
1929	711 Eighth Avenue		Gronenberg and Leuchtag
1928	681 Eighth Avenue	Manufacturers Hanover Bank	Dennison and Hirons
1933	52 Grove Street		Matthew W. Del Gaudio
1930	38 Pearl Street	Greek Shipping Line	Warren and Wetmore
1929	691 Madison Avenue	Porters	McKim, Mead, and White
1930	56th Street and Fifth Avenue	Bonwit Teller	Warren and Wetmore
1931	605 West 181st Street	W. T. Grant	P. A. Cunnius
1929	411 Park Avenue South		M. Bunim
1930			Erhard Djorup
1929	1146 St. Nicholas Avenue	Chemical Bank	Alfred Felheimer and S. Wagner
1930	4186 Broadway	Chemical Bank	Alfred Felheimer and S. Wagner

1927	740 Lexington Avenue	Bloomingdale's	George and E. Blum S. Walter Katz
1926	727 Fifth Avenue	Tiffany's	Rouse and Goldstone
1935	1462 First Avenue	Lipkind Shoe Store	Lowinson and Todaro
1932	129 East 45th Street	ZumZum	F. R. Stuckert
1920–1	446 Fifth Avenue	Kress	Edward F. Sibhert John B. Snook and Son
1935			
1933	224 West Fourth Street	Village Reform Democrats	Phelps Barnum
1938	201 West 11th Street	Plants Inc.	Albert Goldhammer
1929	Hoyt, Livingston, and Fulton streets Streets and York Avenue	Abraham and Straus	

HOTELS

1924	48th and 49th streets Lexington Avenue	Shelton Towers	Arthur Loomis
1930	981 Madison Avenue	Carlyle	Sylvan Bien
1929	490 Eighth Avenue	New Yorker	Sugarman and Berger
1928	First Avenue and 49th Street	Beekman	John Mead Howells
1931	301 Park Avenue	Waldorf- Astoria	Schultz and Weaver
1931	228 West 47th Street	Hotel Edison	Herbert J. Krapp
1930	106 Central Park South	Barbizon Plaza	Murgatroyd and Ogden
1938	150 Central Park South	South Hampshire House	J. M. Felson

HIGH-RISE APARTMENTS

1931	740 Park Avenue		Rosario Candela
1930	115 Central Park West	Century	Irwin S. Chanin

1930	300 Central Park West	El Dorado	Margon and Holder
1936	19 East 88th Street		W. M. Dowling
1930	55 Central Park West		Schwartz and Gross
1929	7 Gracie Square		George B. Post and Sons
1931	320 Central Park West	Ardsley	Emery Roth and Sons
1935	411 West End Avenue		George Fred Pelham
1931	7 West 96th Street		Thomas W. Lamb
1930	49 East 96th Street		Thomas W. Lamb
1928–29	138 East 38th Street	Tower Apartments (originally YWCA)	Francis Y. Joannes
1925	19 East 83d Street		Mott Schmidt
1932	310 East 55th Street		George G. Miller
1930	3 East 84th Street		Joseph Medill Paterson
1931	241 Central Park West		Schwartz and Gross
1929	336 Central Park West		Schwartz and Gross
1936	17 West 54th Street	Rockefeller Apartments	Harrison and Fouilhoux
1930	307 and 310 East 44th Street	Beaux-Arts	Murchison and Hood Godley and Fouilhoux

LOW-RISE HOUSING

1938	2 Grove Street		Irving Margon
1930	433 East 51st Street		Emery Roth
1929	235 East 22d Street		George and Edward Blum
1929	210 East 68th Street		George and Edward Blum
1938	200 West 20th Street	Kensington	Emery Roth
1939–40	252 East 61st Street		Horace Ginsbern
C. 1933	205 West 15th Street		
C. 1925	530 East 88th Street		
1941	10 Downing Street		Steven L. Heidrick
1942	4395 Broadway		Theodore E. Heindsmann

1940	110 Bennett Avenue		Horace Ginsbern
1929	105 Arden at Broadway		Moore and Landisidel
1929	4700 Broadway		Cohen and Siegel
1936			Herbert Lilien
1937			Sugarman and Berger
1951	60 East Ninth Street 155 West 20th Street	Hamilton	H. I. Feldman
1937	151st to 153d Streets and Seventh Avenue	Harlem River Houses	Archibald Brown Horace Ginsbern Charles F. Fuller Richard W. Buckley John Wilson Frank J. Forster Will R. Amon
1926–30	Grand, Broome, Willett, and Lewis Streets	Hillman Houses	Springsteen and Goldhammer

RELIGIOUS BUILDINGS

1929	1 East 65th Street	Temple Emanu-El	Robert D. Kohn Charles Butler Clarence S. Stein
1929	90th Street and Fifth Avenue	Episcopal Heavenly Rest	Mayers, Murray, and Philip
1930	250 East 61st Street	Trinity Baptist	Martin Hedmark
1929	14th Street between Sixth and Seventh Avenues	Salvation Army	Voorhees, Gmelin, and Walker
1928	Broadway at 172d Street	United Methodist Church	

SCHOOLS

1940	Park Avenue–68th and 69th Streets	Hunter College	Shreve, Lamb, and Harmon and Harrison and Fouilhoux

| 1930 | 66 West 12th Street | New School for Social Research | Joseph Urban |
| 1941 | Grand Concourse, Bronx | Cardinal Hayes High School | Eggers and Higgins |

PRISONS AND FEDERAL BUILDINGS

1938	Plaza Street and Flatbush Avenue	Brooklyn Public Library	
1927–32	10 Greenwich Avenue	Women's House of Detention	B. W. Levitan
1936	635 River Avenue	Bronx House of Detention	
1939	Criminal Courthouse	Tombs	Harvey Wiley Corbett
1928	427 West Street	Federal House of Detention	William M. Farrar
1927	40 Worth Street	(Merchant Square Building) State Building	Hill and Murdock
1935	125 Worth Street	Health Building	E. Meyers

HOSPITALS

1933	68th to 70th Streets and York Avenue	New York Hospital	Coolidge, Shepley, Bulfinch, and Abbott
1932	444 East 68th Street	Kerbs	Coolidge, Shepley, Bulfinch, and Abbott
1935	440 East 68th Street	Sloan-Kettering Cancer Center	James Gamble Rogers
1928	622–630 West 168th Street	Columbia-Presbyterian	James Gamble Rogers
1931	50 Haven Avenue	Columbia-Bard Hall	James Gamble Rogers
1928	40 East 61st Street	Le Roy	Kenneth Franzhe

| 1930 | Seventh and Greenwich Avenues | St. Vincent's Lowenstein Pavilion | |
| 1928 | Broadway and 196th Street | Jewish Memorial Hospital | Charles B. Myers Alfred Felheimer |

RESTAURANTS AND GARAGES

1931	607 West 181st Street	Horn and Hardart	P. A. Cunnius
1939	20 Mott Street	China Lane	Arnold W. Lederer
c.1933	600 West 49th Street	Munson Diner	
1927	28 East 63d Street	Restaurant Passy	M. Gerade
c.1930	406 East 91st Street Greenwich and Exchange Alley	Parking Garage City Parking	Horace Ginsbern

PRIVATE RESIDENCES

| 1931 | 120 East 64th Street | | Simeon B. Eisendrath |
| 1930 | 10 East 93d Street | | Roswell and Barrett |

THEATERS

1928–36	181st Street and Broadway	R.K.O. Coliseum	E. Derosa Otto H. Spin Elwyn E. Seelye
1930	175th Street and Broadway	Loew's	Thomas Lamb
1931	1260 Sixth Avenue	Radio City Music Hall	

BRIDGES AND HIGHWAYS

| 1931 | | George Washington Bridge | O. H. Ammann |

159

| 1929–31 | | West Side Highway | Cass Gilbert |
| 1936 | West and Prince Streets | Dock | J. C. Collyer (engineer in charge) |

ZOO

| 1935 | Brooklyn | Prospect Park Zoo | Aymar Embury II |

SUBWAY

| 1931 | Bridge and Willoughby Streets | BMT Ironwork | Voorhees, Gmelin, and Walker |

9

LISTING OF ART DECO BUILDINGS ARRANGED BY LOCATION

ABBREVIATIONS OF BUILDING FUNCTIONS

OS   Office skyscraper
PR   Private residence
OWF Office, warehouse, factory
LO   Low office
HA   High-rise apartment house
HD   Housing development
LA   Low-rise apartment house—ten stories or less
D   Department store
LS   Low store
H   Hotel
F   Federal building
B   Bank
SS   Small shop
S   School
T   Theater
H   Hospital
G   Garage
C   Religious building
R   Restaurant or bar

Downtown Area—Canal to the Battery

F   Outlying pier building. Spring, Canal, West streets. Holland Tunnel
F   Pier building. New York 25. North Moore Street and West Street
OS   125 Barclay Street
OS   New York Telephone. 140 West Street.
R   50 West Street. Cosmo's Bar
OS   Downtown Athletic Club. 18–21 West Street.
F   Brooklyn Battery Tunnel. Triborough World War I Plaza. Battery between Washington and Trinity Streets

G	Triborough Bridge parking garage
OWF	DeBrosses. Roll Color Products
OWF	12–14 DeBrosses Street, Frateli-Branca, Inc.
OWF	205 Hudson Street
OWF	189–195 Hudson Street
OWF	145 Hudson Street at Hubert Street
OWF	99 Hudson Street at Franklin Street
OWF	Western Union Building. 160 West Broadway 60 Hudson Street.
F	Federal Post Office Building
OS	78 Trinity Place. American Stock Exchange
OS	74 Trinity Place
F	Pink Post Office. Southwest corner Church Street and Canal Street
OWF	Bell Telephone Company. Walker and Sixth Avenue
OWF	220 Church Street. New York Human Resources Building
OS	State Insurance Fund Building. Thomas-Duane-Church Streets
LS	Wally Frank Building. Warren Street and Church Street
OS	99 Church Street
B	East River Savings Bank. Church, Dey, Cortlandt Streets.
B	First National City Bank. Broadway and Canal Street. 401 Broadway
LS	351-353-355 Broadway
OS	165 Church Street
B	265–267 Broadway. Chemworks Building
OS	253 Broadway. Home Life Insurance
OS	37 Broadway. Lamston
OS	29 Broadway at Morris Street.
OS	50 Broadway. Underwriters Trust Building
OS	Irving Trust Building. 1 Wall Street at Broadway.
OS	Southeast corner John Street and Broadway
OS	Southeast corner Fulton Street and Broadway
LS	402-404-406 Broadway
F	Health Building. Center Street and Worth Street, northwest
F	Municipal Building. Center Street and Duane Street
OS	129 Fulton Street
OS	17 John Street
OS	Bankers Trust. Wall, Pine, Nassau Streets
OS	44 Broad Street
OS	80 Broad Street
F	Criminal Courts Building and prison. Between Center, White, Baxter, and Leonard streets.
F	State Building. Center Street and Worth Street, northeast
OS	111 Fulton Street. Aetna Casualty and Life

OS	60 John Street
OS	210 Pine Street. Chemical Bank
OS	40 Wall Street. Originally Bank of the Manhattan Company.
OS	43–45 Broad Street. American Bureau of Shipping 37 Broad Street.
OS	51 Broad Street. Commodity Exchange
LO	38 Pearl Street, Greek Line Building.
LO	78 Broad Street.
R	20 Mott Street. China Lane Restaurant
F	United States Post Office. Southeast corner Water and Peck Streets.
OS	99 John Street
OS	111 John Street.
OS	80 John Street. Travelers Insurance
OS	90 John Street
OS	116 John Street
OS	102 Maiden Lane. American International Building 100 Maiden Lane
OS	60 Wall Tower. 70 Pine Street.
OS	63 Wall Street. Brown Brothers. Harriman Building
OS	65 Beaver Street
OS	76 Beaver Street
OS	120 Wall Street
OS	99 Wall Street
F	United States Assay Building. Old Slip at South Street.
HD	Knickerbocker Village. Catherine to Market Streets, Cherry to Monroe Streets.

Village East and West

OWF	Tenth Avenue between 16th and 17th Streets.
OWF	75 Ninth Avenue. Manhattan Industrial Center
OWF	14th Street and Tenth Avenue.
G	New York Post Office Parking Garage. St. John's Building
F	Ventilation Building. Canal and Washington Streets.
OWE	76 Ninth Avenue. Port of New York Building 111 Eighth Avenue. Port of New York Building Con Ed Blockhouse. Greenwich Avenue and 13th Street
LA	227 West 13th Street
HA	2 Greenwich at 13th Street
G	247 West 12th Street, Mercedes Parking
LA	16 Jane Street
T	Greenwich Theater. Greenwich Street and 12th Street
HA	302 Eighth Avenue.
LA	75 Bank Street. Abingdon Court

LA	101 Perry Street
G	232 Eleventh Avenue Manhattan Seventh-Day Adventist Church
LA	247 West 10th Street
LS	224 West 4th Street at Sheridan Square
HA	95 Christopher Street
LA	25 Christopher Street
LS	52 Grove Street
	88 Seventh Avenue. Tamawa Club
LA	2 Grove Street. Between Hudson and Barrow Streets.
F	324 Spring Street. Port of New York Authority.
OWF	Morton and Greenwich Building
OWF	435 Hudson Street
OWF	345 Hudson Street
R	179 Varick Street. Restaurant and bar
	175 Varick Street
OWF	153 Varick Street
OWF	131 Varick Street
OWF	121 Varick Street at Dominick Street
F	Holland Tunnel Blockhouse and Entrance. Watts between Hudson Street and Seventh Avenue
OWF	250 Hudson Street
LA	335 West 19th Street. The Diane
T	Elgin Theater. Eighth Avenue and 19th Street.
HA	56 Seventh Avenue. 1939
HA	123 West Street. Evangeline Residence.
H	St. Vincent's Hospital. Leon Lowenstein Clinic
	St. Vincent's Hospital Residence. 130 West 12th Street
HA	45 Christopher Street
HA	10 Sheridan Square
HA	136 Waverly Place
OWF	333 Sixth Avenue
G	Texaco Parking Garage. Seventh Avenue and Morton Street
HA	241 Sixth Avenue. Breen Towers
G	206 Houston Street. Garage
OWF	200 Varick Street. Empire Color Building
LA	210 West 19th Street
G	236 West 17th Street. Garage.
HA	201 West 16th Street
HA	200 West 16th Street
	121 West 14th Street. Federation of Handicapped
HA	200 West 15th Street.
HA	59 West 12th Street
HA	49 West 12th Street
LA	31 West 8th Street
HA	20 West 9th Street at Fifth Avenue
LS	36–38 West 8th Street
S	8 West Eighth. Old Whitney School
LS	210 Sixth Avenue

164

LS	11–15 East 57th Street
OS	41 East 57th Street. Fuller Building.
LS	55 East 57th Street. Baccarat Building
D	727 Fifth Avenue. Tiffany & Co.
D	Fifth Avenue and 56th Street. Bonwit Teller
OS	Southwest corner Madison Avenue and 57th Street. I.B.M. Building
OS	32 East 57th Street. Pace
OS	38 East 57th Street
OS	56 East 57th Street
OS	515 Madison Avenue
LS	509 Madison Avenue and subway sign and small 2-story low store. 36 East 53d Street
OS	501 Madison Avenue
OS	488 Madison Avenue. Look Building
OS	485 Madison Avenue
OS	424 Madison Avenue
OS	40 East 49th Street and 425 Madison Avenue
OS	420 Madison Avenue
OS	400 Madison Avenue. Gothic variation
OS	19 East 47th Street
	6 East 45th Street. Franklin National Bank Building
OS	19 East 47th Street
LS	340 Madison Avenue. Charles and Company
LO	42d Street and Park Avenue. Airlines Terminal Building
LS	304 Madison Avenue. Goldsmith Brothers
OS	275 Madison Avenue
LS	16 East 41st Street
OS	275 Madison Avenue. Johns-Manville Building
OS	271 Madison Avenue
OS	232 Madison Avenue. Gothic
HO	The Town House. 108 East 38th Street
HA	36 East 36th Street
LA	20 East 35th Street
H	10 Park Avenue
	Southwest corner 180 Madison Avenue
OS	181 Madison Avenue
OS	152 Madison Avenue
OS	2 Park Avenue
OS	425 Park Avenue
OS	419 Park Avenue
LS	411 Park Avenue. Kaye Color Corporation.
OS	79 Madison Avenue
OS	386 Park Avenue
OS	724 Fifth Avenue
B	Southwest corner 52d Street and Fifth Avenue. First National City Bank
OS	Rockefeller Center
OS	4 West 49th Street. Swiss Center Building
OS	French Building. 551 Fifth Avenue
OS	Lefcourt National Building. 521 Fifth Avenue
OS	500 Fifth Avenue

LS   446 Fifth Avenue.. Kress
OS   40 West 40th Street. American Radiator Building
LS   445 Fifth Avenue. Woolworth
OS   350 Fifth Avenue. Empire State Building
OS   307 Fifth Avenue
OS   281 Fifth Avenue
OS   261 Fifth Avenue

West Midtown

LO   Between 58th and 59th Streets at Eleventh
      Avenue. Buick/Opal
F   Between 55th and 56th Streets at West.
      Department of Sanitation
S   850 Tenth Avenue. John Jay Law School
HO   650 West 54th Street
HO   619 West 54th Street. Movie Cab Building
HO   601 West 54th Street
OWF   650 Eleventh Avenue. Porsche-Audi
OWF   635 Eleventh Avenue
OWF   636 Eleventh Avenue
OWF   560 West 42d Street
LS   501 West 42d Street
OWF   501 Tenth Avenue
F   Entrance to Lincoln Tunnel. 38th Street and
      Tenth Avenue
LS   422 Eleventh Avenue
OWF   460 West 34th Street. Office warehouse
F   341 Ninth Avenue. Parcel Post Building
F   303 Ninth Avenue. District Health Center
F   28th Street and Tenth Avenue. Park Walls
HD   24th Street between Ninth and Tenth Avenues.
      London Terrace
OWF   255 Eleventh Avenue. Starrett-Lehigh Building
OWF   524 West 23d Street. Itkins Warehouse
OS   1775 Broadway. Old General Motors Building
LO   959 Eighth Avenue. Hearst Building
G   53d and 54th Streets on Eighth Avenue. Municipal
      Parking Garage
LS   766 Eighth Avenue
LS   725 Eighth Avenue. Century Pawnbrokers
OS   630 Ninth Avenue. Film Center Building
      711 Eighth Avenue
H   700 Eighth Avenue. Royal Manhattan Hotel
B   681 Eighth Avenue. Manufacturers Hanover
H   42d and Ninth Avenue. Hotel Holland
OS   330 West 42d Street. McGraw-Hill Building
LS   39th to 40th Streets on Eighth Avenue
LS   555 Eighth Avenue

LS	545 Eighth Avenue
OS	270 West 38th Street. LeBro Building
OS	535 Eighth Avenue
OS	520 Eighth Avenue
OS	370 West 35th Street.
G	325 West 35th Street. Parking garage
OS	505 Eighth Avenue. Sachs Building
OS	519 Eighth Avenue
H	490 Eighth Avenue. Hotel New Yorker. Mayflower Coffee Shop
F	31st and 33d Streets and Eighth Avenue. General Post Office
OS	370 Ninth Avenue. Sears, Roebuck
	400 Eighth Avenue
	252 West 30th Street
	330 Seventh Avenue
	253 West 26th Street
R	204 West 23d Street
HA	208 West 23d Street
LA	255 West 23d Street
LA	255 West 23d Street
LS	Northeast corner Ninth Avenue and 23d Street. Lamston
HA	300 West 23d Street
LA	312–320 West 23d Street. Louis Philippe
HA	240 Central Park South
OS	1776 Broadway. Lazarus Building
OS	200 West 57th Street
LS	1745 Broadway
H	56th Street and Seventh Avenue. Hotel Sheraton
OS	1710 Broadway. ILGWU Building
OS	1657 Broadway
R	1619 Broadway. Jack Dempsey's
LS	50th Street and Seventh Avenue
LS	745 Seventh Avenue
LS	A. S. Beck. 48th and 49th Streets and Seventh Avenue
LS	1576 Broadway. Publicity Building
OS	47th Street and Seventh Avenue. De Mille Building
R	Between 46th and 45th Streets and Sixth Avenue. Horn and Hardart
OS	1501 Seventh Avenue. Times Building
OS	Northeast corner 41st Street and Seventh Avenue
OS	570 Seventh Avenue
OS	575 Seventh Avenue
	1450 Broadway
	598 Seventh Avenue. Black and white columns
	530 Seventh Avenue
OS	533 Seventh Avenue
OS	1407 Broadway
OS	1400 Broadway
OS	512 Seventh Avenue. The Navarre

OS	1375 Broadway. Lefcourt State
OS	1384 Broadway. Lefcourt Normandie.
OS	1001 Sixth Avenue
OS	499 Seventh Avenue
OS	491 Seventh Avenue.
OS	1359 Broadway. Lefcourt Marlboro
OS	360 Sixth Avenue. Lefcourt Empire
	463 Seventh Avenue
OS	1333 Broadway. Johnson Building
OS	1330 Broadway
OS	450 Seventh Avenue. Nelson Tower
B	Northwest corner 34th Street and Seventh Avenue. First National City Bank
LS	363 Seventh Avenue
LS	345 Seventh Avenue
OS	275 Seventh Avenue. ILGWU Health Center
H	Central Park South. Essex House
H	Central Park South. Hampshire House
H	Central Park South. Barbizon Plaza Hotel
R	104 and 106 West 57th Street. Horn and Hardart
OS	57 West 57th Street
LO	37 West 57th Street. Vogar Building
OS	29 West 57th Street
B	3 West 57th Street. Greenwich Savings Bank
LO	50 West 57th Street
LO	22 West 57th Street
HA	17 West 54th Street. Rockefeller Apartments.
F	Bryant Park Blockhouse. Northeast corner Sixth Avenue and 40th Street
LO	1040 Sixth Avenue
LO	Herald Square, 32d and Sixth Avenue. John David Building
LO	Union Dime Historic Site
LO	1216–1220 Broadway. Three-story
	1214 Broadway
LO	1199 Broadway
	1158 Broadway

Upper West Side

HA	685 West End Avenue
HA	565 West End Avenue
HA	140 Riverside Drive
HA	100 Riverside Drive
HA	411 West End Avenue
LA	320 West 76th Street
LA	304 West 75th Street
HA	315 West End Avenue
HA	5 Riverside Drive
LA	300 West 72d Street

170

OWF 125 West End Avenue. New York Times North
     Building
HA   80 West End Avenue
HD   61st and 64th Streets. West End Avenue and
     Amsterdam Houses
OWB 60th and 61st Streets. Firestone Plant
LS   2427 Broadway
T   2409 Broadway. New Yorker theater
HA   400 West End Avenue
LS   201 West 72d Street
HA   244 West 72d Street
P   255 West 71st Street
HA   111 West 94th Street
HA   112 West 94th Street
LA   175 West 93d Street
LA   175 West 92d Street at Amsterdam Avenue
S   154 West 93d Street. Joan of Arc High School
HA   200 West 86th Street
LS   2315 Broadway
HA   142 West 86th Street
G   149 West 83rd Street. Garage
R   103 West 72d Street. Blarney Castle Bar
S   170 West 72d Street. Geneva School of Business
LS   128 West 72d Street
LA   49 West 96th Street
HA   7 West 96th Street
HA   336 Central Park West
HA   320 Central Park West. Ardsley
HA   300 Central Park West. El Dorado
HA   295 Central Park West
HA   57 West 86th Street
HA   5 West 86th Street
HA   40 West 86th Street
C   7 West 83d Street. Rodeph Sholom.
     241 Central Park West
HA   211 Central Park West. Beresford
HA   38 West 72d Street
HA   115 Central Park West. Majestic
HA   55 Central Park West
HA   25 Central Park West. Century
OWF 45 Columbus Avenue. Sofia Warehouse
LO   1860 Broadway

Upper East Side

S   6 East 94th Street
P   10 East 93d Street
C   Church of the Heavenly Rest. 4 East 90th Street
HA   19 East 88th Street

HA	2 East 88th Street at Fifth Avenue
LA	3 East 84th Street
HA	19 East 83d Street
HA	19 East 80th Street
HA	965 Fifth Avenue
HA	955 Fifth Avenue
HA	28 East 73d Street
HA	19 East 72d Street
HA	4 East 72d Street
HA	880 Fifth Avenue
LA	3 East 69th Street.
HA	17 East 67th Street
HA	850 Fifth Avenue
C	Temple Emmanu-El, 1 East 65th Street.
	838 Fifth Avenue. AUX Building.
	654 Madison Avenue. First Empire Bank
HA	49 East 96th Street
LA	48 East 92d Street
HA	1150 Park Avenue
HA	40 East 88th Street
HA	49 East 86th Street
C	50 East 87th Street. Park Avenue Synagogue.
HA	940 Park Avenue
	944 Park Avenue
LS	1049 Madison Avenue
LA	50 East 78th Street
H	981 Madison Avenue
HA	65 East 76th Street
HA	54 East 72d Street
HA	740 Park Avenue.
LS	691–695 Madison Avenue. Porters Building
LA	28 East 63d Street. The Lowell. 1927–34.
	Restaurant Passy.
HA	530 Park Avenue
LA	1372–1378 Lexington Avenue
LA	111 East 88th Street
LA	110 East 87th Street
B	117 East 86th Street. First National City Bank
HA	1001 Park Avenue
HA	895 Park Avenue
LA	203–215 East 88th Street
OWF	1411 Third Avenue. Manhattan Warehouse
LS	Southeast corner 79th Street and Lexington Avenue. Doorway
LA	231 East 76th Street
C	319 East 74th Street. Greek Orthodox Cathedral.
LA	310 East 74th Street
C	218 East 70th Street. United Synagogue
LA	210 East 68th Street
LA	63d Street and Second Avenue
C	250 East 61st Street. Trinity Baptist Church.

S	96th Street and First Avenue. Manhattan Technical High School addition
F	312 East 94th Street. Department of Social Services
LA	207 East 84th Street
LA	350 East 77th Street
LA	310 East 75th Street
LA	402 East 74th Street
LA	330 East 71st Street
LA	331 East 71st Street
LA	Southeast corner 68th Street and Second Avenue
P	315 East 68th Street
OWF	1166 Second Avenue. Day-Murray and Young warehouse
G	304 East 64th Street. Avis Garage
G	406 East 91st Street. Parking garage
F	427 East 87th Street. Post office
LA	420 East 86th Street
P	124 East 70th Street
HA	Park Avenue between 68th and 69th Streets
LA	116 East 68th Street
P	120 East 64th Street
LA	782 Lexington Avenue
HA	505 Park Avenue
LO	742–748 Lexington Avenue. Dry Dock Savings
HA	166 East 96th Street
LA	152 East 94th Street
HCA	1395 Lexington Avenue.
LA	91st and Third Avenue
LA	161 East 88th Street
OWF	158 East 87th Street. Morgan Manhattan Warehouses
G	169–171 East 87th Street. Yorkville Garage
G	152 East 87th Street. Alan Garage
T	Loew's 86th Street Theater. Back side
LA	155 East 77th Street
	177 East 77th Street
LS	1360 Third Avenue
LS	1332 Third Avenue
LA	226 East 74th Street
LA	225 East 74th Street
H	63d Street and Lexington. Barbizon Hotel
LS	767 Lexington Avenue. Lambert Building
D	Lexington Avenue and 60th Street. Bloomingdales
LA	440 East 78th Street
SS	Lipkind Shoes, 1462 First Avenue
G	431 East 75th Street. Garage. Keefe and Keefe
LA	1409 York Avenue
LA	405 East 72d Street
	425 East 72d Street
F	409 East 69th Street. District Health Center

H	444 East 68th Street. Kerbs Memorial Hospital
LA	1161 York Avenue. Sutton Terrace
LO	1114–1116 First Avenue. Schnurmacher Building
LO	410 East 61st Street. Atlas Auto Rental
LA	1700 York Avenue
LA	530 East 88th Street
LA	110 East End Avenue
HA	7 Gracie Square. 1931
LA	9 Gracie Square
LA	1510 York Avenue
P	1410 York Avenue
LO	1334 York Avenue. Eastman Kodak Company
H	New York Hospital

BRONX

HA	1005 Jerome Avenue
HA	2830 Grand Concourse
HA	2488 Grand Concourse
HA	2232 Grand Concourse
HA	1939 Grand Concourse
HA	1675 Grand Concourse
HA	1750 Grand Concourse
HA	1675 Grand Concourse
HA	1035 Grand Concourse
HA	888 Grand Concourse
HA	910 Grand Concourse
HA	930 Grand Concourse
HA	1150 Grand Concourse
HA	1166 Grand Concourse
HA	1188 Grand Concourse
HA	1500 Grand Concourse
	2557 Marion Avenue
	2550 Marion Avenue
S	Cardinal Hayes High School. Grand Concourse
F	Bronx Federal House of Detention.

10

SOURCES

BOOKS

Abbott, Berenice, photographer; text by Elizabeth McCausland, *Changing New York*. New York: E. P. Dutton, 1939.

Andrews, Wayne, *Architecture in New York: A Photographic History*. New York: Harper & Row, 1973.

Bayer, Herbert, and Walter and Ise Gropius, eds., *Bauhaus 1919–1928*. New York: Museum of Modern

Black Mary, ed., *Old New York in Photographs, 1853–1901*. New York: Dover, 1973.

Blake, Peter, *The Master Builders*. New York: Alfred A. Knopf, 1960.

Bush-Brown, Albert, *Louis Sullivan*. New York: George Braziller, 1960.

Busignani, Alberto, *Gropius*. New York: Hamlyn, 1973.

Caramel, Luciano, and Alberto Longatti, *Antonio Sant' Elia*. Como: Villa Comunale Dell 'olmo-como, 1962.

Drexler, Arthur, *Ludwig Mies Van Der Rohe*. New York: George Braziller, 1960.

Gropius, Walter, *The New Architecture and the Bauhaus*. Cambridge, Mass.: M.I.T. Press, 1965.

Hilberseimer, Ludwig, *Mies Van der Rohe*. Chicago: Paul Theobald and Company, 1956.

Hillier, Bevis, *The World of Art Deco*. New York: E. P. Dutton, 1971.

Hitchcock, Henry Russell, and Philip Johnson, *The International Style: Architecture Since 1922*. New York: W. W. Norton, 1932.

Hodeir, Andre, *Jazz: Its Evolution and Essence*. New York: Grove Press, 1939.

Holmes, Judith, *Olympiad 1936: Blaze of Glory for Hitler's Reich.* New York: Ballantine Books, 1971.

Howard, Ebenezer, *Garden Cities of Tomorrow.* Cambridge, Mass.: M.I.T. Press, 1965.

Lenning, Henry F., *The Art Nouveau.* The Hague: Martinus Nijhoff, 1951.

Lyon, Danny, *The Destruction of Lower Manhattan.* New York: Macmillan, 1969.

McClinton, Katherine Morrison, *Art Deco: A Guide for Collectors.* New York: Clarkson N. Potter, 1972.

MacDonald, William, *Early Christian and Byzantine Architecture.* New York: George Braziller, 1965.

Menten, Theodore, ed., *The Art Deco Style in Household Objects, Architecture, Sculpture, Graphics, Jewelry.* New York: Dover, 1972.

O' Gorman, James F., *The Architecture of Frank Furness.* Philadelphia: Philadelphia Museum of Art, 1973.

Selz, Peter, and Mildred Constantine, *Art Nouveau.* New York: Museum of Modern Art, 1959.

Sharp, Dennis, *Modern Architecture and Expressionism.* New York: George Braziller, 1966.

Silver, Nathan, *Lost New York.* Boston: Houghton Mifflin, 1967.

Stewart, Desmond, *Early Islam.* New York: Time-Life Books, 1967.

Valles, J. Prats, ed., *Le Corbusier;* Preface, *"Gaudi,"* Editorial Room. Barcelona: Paseo San Gervasio, 1958.

Von Eckardt, Wolf, *Eric Mendelsohn.* New York: George Braziller, 1960.

White, Norval and Elliot Willensky, eds., *AIA Guide to New York City.* New York: Macmillan, 1967.

Wright, Frank Lloyd, *The Future of Architecture.* New York: Horizon Press, 1953.

BROCHURES AND PAMPHLETS

Lehman, Arnold, L., "1930's Exposition Catalogue." New York Cultural Center, 1973.

"New York City Landmarks." New York: Landmarks Preservation Commission (Harmon H. Goldstone, Chairman).

"New York's New Architecture." New York: Fortune Time-Life.

Sětlik, Jiři and Olga Herbenová, eds., "90 A Jedna Židle." Praha: Uměleckoprumyslove Muzeum, 1972.

Vreeland, Diana, Stella Blum, and Shari Gruhn, "The '10s, the '20's, the '30's Inventive Clothes 1909–1939." New York: The Metropolitan Museum of Art, 1974.

PERIODICALS AND NEWSPAPERS

Goldberger, Paul, "Art Deco, Style Modern—Kitsch or Serious—Is in Vogue," *New York Times,* January 31, 1974, L 35.

Huxtable, Ada Louise, "The Skyscraper Style," *New York Times Magazine,* April 14, 1974.

Lehman, Arnold, "New York Skyscrapers: The Jazz Modern Neo-American Beautilitarian Style," Metropolitan Museum of Art *Bulletin,* April 1971, pp. 363–370.

Morgan, James D., "A Tale of Two Towers, Architecture Plus," *The International Magazine of Architecture,* October 1973, pp. 42–83.

Peck, Richard, "Art Deco, The Newest 'Antique'," *House Beautiful,* August 1973, pp. 61–65.

Plummer, Kathleen Church, "The Streamlined Modern," *Art in America,* January–February 1974, pp. 46–54.

Reif, Rita, "Antiques: Art Deco Style," New York Times, September 8, 1973.

Varian, Elayne, "Art Deco," *The Art Gallery Magazine,* January 1973, pp. 17–23.

Von Eckardt, Wolf, "Rockefeller 'Cathedral': In the '30's, They Knew How to Have Fun," *Washington Post,* February 9, 1974, B 1.

Index

350 89